## More Praise for *The End of Diversity as We Know It*

"This is a results book. It provides a practical guide for committed leaders interested in achieving optimal results through the efforts of people. It is also a handbook for leaders who aspire to do the 'right things right and at the right time.'"

**—Charlie W. Hill, Executive Vice President of Human Resources (retired), Landmark Communications, Inc.**

"In plain English, Martin Davidson explains how diversity can make a company more efficient and innovative, which leads to greater profits. This book artfully blends psychology, social issues, and good business sense to provide baggage-free, 21st-century solutions to problems. Read it before your competitors do."

**—Reginald Hudlin, producer/director and former President, Black Entertainment Television, Inc.**

"Martin Davidson reminds us that diversity is not about others; rather, it is about us and our willingness to push ourselves to the edge of personal discomfort in order to run productive, sustainable institutions; create communities of harmony; and live fuller, happier lives."

**—Subha V. Barry, Chief Diversity Officer and Senior Vice President, Office of Diversity, Inclusion, and Community Engagement, Freddie Mac**

"Martin Davidson hit the nail on the head! This extensively researched book moves the diversity paradigm from the human resource cubicle to the whole organization, the tactical to the strategic, the short term to the sustainable, and the domestic to the global. A must-read for every business leader."

**—Dr. Austin Ifedirah, President and CEO, Aegis Healthcare Holdings, Inc.**

"This is a tactical book for business leaders who know they have to shift their thinking but have never quite understood how (and truthfully, why) to do it. Every CEO who looks at his or her company's diversity initiative and wonders why it hasn't made as much progress should read this book."

**—Todd G. Sears, Principal, Coda Leadership Consulting LLC, and former Americas Head of Diversity & Inclusion, Credit Suisse**

"Professor Davidson takes us on an enlightening journey that raises the bar for any business executive seeking to improve productivity. Leveraging difference is a critical tool for those who are result and not process oriented when deploying talent."

**—Mark Settles, Managing Director, JPMorgan Chase & Co.**

# The End of Diversity As We Know It

# The End of Diversity As We Know It

## Why Diversity Efforts Fail and How Leveraging Difference Can Succeed

MARTIN N. DAVIDSON

BK

Berrett–Koehler Publishers, Inc.
San Francisco
*a BK Business book*

Berrett-Koehler Publishers, Inc.
235 Montgomery Street, Suite 650
San Francisco, CA 94104-2916
Tel: (415) 288-0260 Fax: (415) 362-2512
www.bkconnection.com



**Ordering Information**
**Quantity sales.** Special discounts are available on quantity purchases by corporations, associations, and others. For details, contact the "Special Sales Department" at the Berrett-Koehler address above.
**Individual sales.** Berrett-Koehler publications are available through most bookstores. They can also be ordered directly from Berrett-Koehler: Tel: (800) 929-2929; Fax: (802) 864-7626; www.bkconnection.com.
**Orders for college textbook/course adoption use.** Please contact Berrett-Koehler: Tel: (800) 929-2929; Fax: (802) 864-7626.
**Orders by U.S. trade bookstores and wholesalers.** Please contact Ingram Publisher Services: Tel: (800) 509-4887; Fax: (800) 838-1149; E-mail: customer.service@ingrampublisherservices.com; or visit www.ingrampublisherservices.com/Ordering for details about electronic ordering.

Berrett-Koehler and the BK logo are registered trademarks of Berrett-Koehler Publishers, Inc.

Printed in the United States of America

Berrett-Koehler books are printed on long-lasting acid-free paper. When it is available, we choose paper that has been manufactured by environmentally responsible processes. These may include using trees grown in sustainable forests, incorporating recycled paper, minimizing chlorine in bleaching, or recycling the energy produced at the paper mill.

**Library of Congress Cataloging-in-Publication Data**
Davidson, Martin N.
The end of diversity as we know it : why diversity efforts fail and how leveraging difference can succeed / by Martin N. Davidson.
p. cm.
Includes bibliographical references and index.
ISBN 978-1-60509-343-7 (hardcover : alk. paper)
1. Diversity in the workplace. 2. Corporate culture. I. Title.
HF5549.5.M5D38 2012
658.3008--dc23
2011034022

First Edition
15 14 13 12 10 9 8 7 6 5 4 3 2

Project management, design, and composition by Steven Hiatt / Hiatt & Dragon, San Francisco.
Copyediting: Phyllis Elving Proofreading: Tom Hassett Cover design: Irene Morris
Cover photo: Christopher David Photography

I dedicate this book to my father and mother,
Arlanda and Jean Davidson

# Contents

# Introduction

# A New Possibility for Difference

What does it take to create an organization that can do this?

> Multinational manufacturer Procter & Gamble's business is innovation. With more than $2.9 billion in annual sales in Canada, the company is constantly trying to improve its products and develop new ones. The global business service unit at P&G in Canada is in charge of designing business solutions and is composed of about 150 multifunctional professionals. They come from more than 40 nations, including Venezuela, Japan, Israel, and Ghana, and speak more than 20 languages.
>
> To build and foster a culture of innovation, P&G has entrenched diversity as a key principle in the workplace and leveraged the skilled immigrant talent pool. When faced with the challenge of offshoring and outsourcing in 2002, group members realized, if they wanted to keep their jobs in Canada, they needed to adapt and leverage this diversity in a way no one else could. Now, the global business service unit in Canada has a unique position within the company. It is one of only four groups in the

world devoted to sourcing and supporting P&G services such as IT, employee benefits and payroll, business analytics, and purchasing on a global scale.

In addition to creating a diverse employee mix internally, P&G is open to and prides itself on collaboration with external partners. It has formalized this strategy through its Connect and Develop program. Historically, P&G's best innovations came from connecting ideas across internal businesses. Taking this one step further, the company decided to set a goal to acquire 50 percent of innovations from outside the company. The move was not meant to displace P&G's own staff, but to leverage them by exposing them to even more diverse ideas, people and products. P&G can now identify promising ideas throughout the world and apply its own research and development, manufacturing, marketing, and purchasing capabilities to create better and cheaper products faster.

P&G's leaders turned difference into advantage in other ways as well. It was quickly apparent they could only meet their growth goals through a combination of organic growth and growth through acquisition. They decided that these did not have to be disparate activities. Indeed, they realized that learning could be bidirectional. [1]

This description of Proctor and Gamble Canada was excerpted from an article entitled "Companies Embrace Power of Diversity." As the title suggests, the goal of the story was to highlight the importance of diversity in organizations. But this is not the typical diversity story, the one extolling the virtues of inclusion and highlighting a variety of diversity best practices like targeted hiring, employee networks, and mentoring. This one is different.

First, this diversity story starts with the company's overarching strategy. P&G is an innovation company and it focuses on the kinds of diversity that help it to be a better innovation company. As a result, the article never mentions race, gender, sexual orientation, or age. It's not that these differences don't support innovation. But P&G Canada is much more focused in its approach to diversity of talent. It emphasizes national cultural diversity as most critical to supporting its strategic imperative to innovate in this particular business context. It seems that P&G Canada has a larger goal than simply being an employer of choice for people of various diverse backgrounds.

That larger goal becomes more apparent through initiatives such as the Connect and Develop program. It is designed to cultivate internal and external partner relationships as a way of generating new ways to think about the business. The idea is that supporting diverse collaborations that extend beyond normal corporate boundaries can create even stronger, more innovative results. The program has helped the company apply its innovative process in creating products all over the world.

Diversity is also evident in P&G Canada's growth strategy. Company leaders recognized that cultivating new partnerships would infuse the organization with tangible resources and novel perspectives that would help it grow and compete more sustainably.

In sum, this diversity story is really about how P&G Canada capitalizes on difference in the broadest terms. The company connects with globally diverse stakeholders, and it *uses* those stakeholders to create value in unique and powerful ways.

The breadth of the P&G Canada example surfaces an uncomfortable truth about traditional methods of managing diversity: they don't usually go far enough to really make companies better.

In many organizations, the indicators of whether diversity efforts are successful have been how many people from group X are hired or promoted or fired, or how much product is sold to group Y. This approach doesn't begin to do justice to the potentially positive effect that differences can have on an organization like P&G Canada. The real value of diversity emerges when exploring difference becomes standard operating procedure. Organizations that excell in the global marketplace aren't thinking of diversity as a tangential activity handled by the HR department. Rather, diversity is mission critical. Differences are present—among employees, customers, suppliers, local communities, acquired or acquiring organizations, and governments. Success comes not from shying away from these differences, but from fiercely and skillfully capitalizing on them.

Traditional ways of managing diversity won't always help leaders take advantage of those differences. In fact, sometimes these approaches actually cause problems that destroy, rather create, value. This book is about how organizations can thrive by making the most of the diversity that is right there among their stakeholders. The "Leveraging Difference" approach is designed to foster superior firm performance, both in the present and the future. Drawing on examples from organizations in the United States and around the world, my goal is to guide readers in moving from traditional methods of managing diversity to fully leveraging difference.

## My First Glimpse into Leveraging Difference

A few years back, I worked with members of the leadership team of a Fortune 50 company. The focus was on developing leadership abilities, and I had designed a curriculum that emphasized the role of diversity in leadership. I confess I was more than a little intimidated. Here I was, an untenured (that is, expendable) faculty member preparing to work with a group of thirty-five executives, of whom thirty-three were senior white males, one was a white woman, and one was a multiracial male. I worried that most of them were fairly jaded when it came to diversity and would be bracing themselves for more of the same old rhetoric. I really wanted to make my sessions engaging and stimulating, and I wasn't sure I knew quite how to do so.

Over a four-day period, I spent time with them in four sessions of about ninety minutes each, interspersed between presentations on other topics by two colleagues. My first session went fine. The material was strong, I thought, and I also felt that I was working with a tailwind. This group was energized, upbeat, and excited about engaging in new ideas—in part, I realized, because of some great classes they'd already taken with my colleagues. Thanks to that bonding experience, they were open and ready for learning. By the way, this was in stark contrast to the usual modus operandi for the group. This was a high-performing company that generated terrific results in its industry, but theirs was not a culture of positivity or high energy. They did a job, did it well, and moved on to the next task, all the while critiquing why the job done well hadn't been done better.

My second and third classes with them were also okay, though certainly not great. My prediction at the time was that the leaders would evaluate the sessions as "fine" (and then critique them) but that our time together would have little lasting impact on them.

And then something happened.

The company's CEO stopped by to speak to the group. This was routine for such programs. This CEO was renowned as a strong and thoughtful leader who held his people accountable for results. His task here was to share some of what he had learned by taking the program a year earlier (before I was part of it). He began to speak about the benefits he'd derived from the program, and then—to the surprise of many—he wandered into a critique of leadership development programs like the one we were part of at that moment. His question wasn't whether our program was good or bad (he thought it was quite good), but rather whether such deep explorations into learning and leadership weren't actually indulgences that distracted from the real business at hand: bottom-line results. He proceeded to lay down the company's law of performance and to remind everyone that they were accountable for results.

When he'd finished speaking a half hour later, the group sat in stunned silence. After a few moments, people engaged in polite and sometimes challenging Q&A, but mostly they sat glassy-eyed. The CEO had left me fairly speechless, too. But I figured that was just how things worked in this company, and I left to prepare for my next day's class.

When I showed up the next morning, the buoyant, energetic group of executives I had been working with all week now sat dejected and disengaged. We went through the motions until, disturbed by this marked shift in mood, I called time out and asked what was wrong. Needless to say, it was all about the CEO's talk the prior afternoon. People expressed their disappointment and sadness about what they had heard. They felt duped and resentful about having really opened up to new possibilities, only to have their sponsor slap them down. Indeed, some confessed to having felt the need to drown their sorrows in a drink or two the night before.

As I listened, something occurred to me. I had worked with one of the company's African American employee resource networks. In the unit I'd visited, younger African American employees had been struggling, and turnover was unusually high. I had been struck by how these conscientious and committed young professionals were convinced they couldn't be successful in this company because of its difficult culture. Now, as I looked at these executives, I was struck by how much they resembled those disenfranchised African American employees. Both groups were de-motivated and unhappy. Both were frustrated and resentful. I shared my observation and summarized by saying, "You know, in this moment you are just like the black people in your company, the very same people that are the source of concern and consternation to so many of your managers."

They were shocked. To be honest, so was I. But the connection seemed critical for them, and in retrospect it was critical for me as well. The essential insight from my conversation with that mostly white, mostly male group was that they actually had a great deal in common with their African American employees. What they all shared was a common experience of how people were managed in the company. The firm's style and culture had a distinct effect on its people, and while some of that was constructive—they were high performing—some of it was not.

The relentless focus on results to the exclusion of empowering, appreciating, and celebrating the people who created those results was detrimental—even toxic—for many. And the black employees were the "canaries in the coal mine." They were the ones who, by virtue of being marginalized in the company, were more vulnerable to this negative side of management style. When they voiced the challenges they felt around the lack of employee empowerment and autonomy, and the diminished opportunity to advance, they were highlighting a vulnerability that *every* employee in that company faced, regardless of race.

Until that moment, these executives had operated under the illusion that they would never have the same disempowering experience those black junior employees had. That illusion was now over. Everyone was in it together.

Several years later, this company has evolved, and its culture and management style are shifting. Not surprisingly, this has been fueled by leadership transitions and by the influence of newly acquired companies from around the globe. But in my time with that group of leaders, I caught a glimpse of why difference is so critically important for organizations. The new perspective—the extraordinary dissent—emerges because there is an opportunity for improvement and a need to change the status quo. It is the critical resource for helping organizations to innovate and operate more effectively. And the ability to look for and listen to these different perspectives—or to proactively solicit them—is one of several core skills that I'll expand upon in this book.[2]

## Overview and Roadmap for the Book

Traditional diversity efforts—in this book I call them "Managing Diversity"—focus on recruiting and integrating people who represent a varied but limited set of diverse identities. Following the Hudson Institute's prescient "Workforce 2000" report in 1987 forecasting dramatic demographic changes in the U.S. workforce,[3] organizations have evolved numerous Managing Diversity initiatives to help them deal with this new workforce. These initiatives have had a significant impact over the past two decades. The best ones have made organizations more welcoming for traditionally excluded people and helped companies enter new and diverse markets. But even the best of these initiatives are now falling short of solving the challenges of competing in the complex modern marketplace because they unduly narrow the potential impact difference can have on an organization.

Traditional diversity efforts frequently emphasize how to develop workplaces in which people with different perspectives and identities work well together despite (and because of) their differences. For example, Northrop Grumman Corporation, one of DiversityInc's "Top 50 Companies for Diversity," has as its diversity and inclusion goal "to attract, develop, and retain the best and brightest from all walks of life and backgrounds. This requires an organization to have a culture of inclusion where all individuals feel respected, are treated fairly, provided work-life balance, and an opportunity to excel in their chosen careers."[4] PricewaterhouseCoopers, the third-ranked company on DiversityInc's list, states that its "diversity initiatives and strategies are designed to attract, develop, and advance the most talented individuals regardless of their race, sexual orientation, religion, age, gender, or any other dimension of diversity."[5]

This goal of attracting and engaging employees with varied identities and perspectives is a necessary part of any significant diversity initiative. But it isn't sufficient in itself to take full advantage of what those differences can offer. Organizations that truly leverage difference cultivate the capability to engage with and learn from diverse stakeholders, including employees, customers, partners, and communities. They use what they learn to explore how they can do the work of their organization more effectively. They are able to apply lessons of difference to domains as wide-ranging as customer engagement, operational procedures, and alliances with community resources. With time, these organizations can become "difference factories." But first leaders must move beyond thinking about diversity simply as race, gender, culture or personality differences. In the following chapters we will explore the larger mosaic and begin to map out how leaders and organizations can leverage the many kinds of difference that might make a difference to their businesses.

The first chapter—"The End of Diversity as We Know It"—argues that traditional approaches to diversity (those we call Managing Diversity) are not very effective in contemporary organizations. Drawing on the best research in the field, it takes on some diversity sacred cows and outlines when diversity helps and when it doesn't. It then highlights shortcomings in the Managing Diversity approach that are tough to admit but that need to be discussed. The second chapter, "The Beginning of Leveraging Difference," introduces a remedy and shows how the Managing Diversity approach or "frame" differs from what I call "Leveraging Difference." Managing Diversity is not an inherently bad way to deal with difference—it has often been effective in past decades. But it isn't going to be effective in the coming decades. A new frame is necessary: Leveraging Difference.

In chapter 3, "The Leveraging Difference Capability," co-author Heather Wishik and I begin to define how organizations can apply Leveraging Difference to change the way they operate. One of the shortcomings of the Managing Diversity approach was that it wasn't well integrated into organizational strategy; in most cases it was either a component of or a tactical add-on to HR management. Conceiving of Leveraging Difference as strategic for the entire organization moves diversity to center stage and makes it the job of every manager and leader, not just an HR diversity specialist.

Developing that Leveraging Difference capability requires moving through a cycle of seeing, understanding, and engaging difference, and we use a detailed case from Wipro Technologies to show Leveraging Difference in action.

Chapter 4, "Seeing Difference," describes the first phase of the cycle in detail. This is the point at which leaders identify what differences are likely to be strategically relevant for them. Key competencies for seeing difference are discussed, including understanding the enterprise strategy, having a mindset that assumes that differences are there (and do affect the organization), and managing the filters and biases that keep us from seeing difference accurately. Chapter 5, "Understanding Difference," explores the point at which leaders learn how those differences are affecting the organization, and how they might enhance bottom-line results. I also discuss how learning is accelerated when leaders build healthy relationships across difference and learn to manage charged emotions and conflict that can emerge in those relationships. And finally the chapter discusses ways to build systems in organizations that provide information about relevant differences whenever needed.

The last part of the Leveraging Difference cycle is discussed in chapter 6, "Engaging Difference." This is when knowledge is translated into coordinated action. Engaging difference projects are experiments that allow organizations to explore ways to use relevant difference to generate results. The case studies in this chapter, co-authored with Heather Wishik, show organizations as they move through the three stages of the cycle: seeing, understanding, and engaging difference.

Chapter 7, "Discovering Leveraging Difference," offers insight into what organizations that have developed a Leveraging Difference capability look like, and it describes in more depth the dynamic quality of the cycle. It explains what leaders can do to help organizations shift from simply conducting successful engaging difference experiments here and there to truly implementing a Leveraging Difference capability.

The book's epilogue, "The Power of the Margin," addresses more directly the challenge of not dismissing intractable differences like race, gender, or sexual orientation because they appear not to be strategically relevant differences. Rather than breathing a sigh of relief at being able to avoid these perplexing differences, leaders should engage them eagerly. Each country and culture has it "hot spot" differences, the ones that are most emotionally charged and difficult to come to terms with. These could be precisely the differences that can help organizations learn to develop their Leveraging Difference capability most effectively.

## Who This Book Can Help

I wrote this book for an unusually disparate audience of leaders. I believe that it can help senior executives, middle managers, chief learning officers, human resource professionals, corporate diversity professionals, and management consultants—especially those who focus on diversity. I don't subscribe to the notion that leaders are found only at the tops of organizations. Leaders are everywhere. Some have titles, some don't. One of the most powerful insights to come from our work with diversity is that leadership often is present in unexpected places, demonstrated by people we didn't think had it in them.

*Senior executives* will be able to use the book as a roadmap to helping create value for their businesses. One of the book's main tenets is that diversity activity should flow from an organization's comprehensive business strategy. Difference is an important but neglected resource that leaders can use in the development and execution of that strategy. Concrete leadership actions are presented for developing an organizational capability for leveraging difference.

*Middle-level managers* can use the book to make sense of the diversity demands their organizations place on them. Having a leadership perspective is incredibly useful, even if you aren't yet a senior leader, and this book can encourage that mindset. From a practical point of view, it offers concrete steps for building positive professional relationships with colleagues, subordinates, and superiors. The techniques that are useful for managing across differences are often just as useful for managing someone you think is just like you.

Dealing with traditional Managing Diversity efforts is often the most challenging for middle managers. It puts pressure on them to operate in ways that aren't always comfortable, and that can breed resistance. This can be especially challenging for managers from majority groups—in the United States, straight white men (in other countries, it might be someone else). This book offers a clear and compelling rationale for being open to learning about groups different from one's own. And it can help majority managers better understand their role in leveraging difference.

*Chief learning officers, human resource and corporate diversity specialists, and diversity consultants*—those tasked with being experts in diversity—can benefit from this book for many of the same reasons as executives and managers. The book offers a new set of tools to help them develop their expertise, and it provides them with useful strategies for influencing their organizational constituents.

## The Research Methodology

Insights and recommendations in this book are based on data from a number of sources. My colleagues and I collected survey and interview data from managers of diverse racial and ethnic backgrounds in a variety of U.S. organizations. In addition, we interviewed senior executives in the Americas, Europe, and Asia as part the Successful Global Leadership Project sponsored by the Batten Institute at the Darden School of Business, University of Virginia. We also conducted in-depth case and action research with more than twenty organizations spanning multiple industries. And we drew on a range of archival data available in the public domain.

In the research we conducted with domestic managers, we examined what practices and processes best create a climate in which managers with diverse identities feel they can succeed. Our survey sample of managers included 133 African Americans, 111 other managers of color, and 244 white managers, for a total of 488. Of those, 34 African American managers (26 percent of those surveyed), 79 white managers (32 percent), 13 Hispanic managers (29 percent), and 8 Asian American managers (12 percent) responded to our survey. We followed up by conducting individual interviews with thirty-two of the managers, half of them white and half managers of color.

To expand our inquiry, we collected interview data from twenty-three senior executives (as well as their superiors and those who report directly to them) as part of the Successful Global Leadership Project. We investigated how globally diverse leaders and companies develop people and practices to leverage differences within their organizations, among customers and markets, and on leadership teams. We examined what they have learned about the processes, assumptions, understandings, and leadership skills that equip leaders and managers to develop critical and strategic relationships. Seven global enterprises were selected for the project, operating in the United States, South America, Europe, Africa, and the Middle East and Asia.

These projects yielded in-depth case material. We were able to collect data on strategy, marketing, product development, client relations, operational effectiveness, and talent management practices for a subset of the organizations. We also drew on our research with multiple organizations noted for effective work involving diversity and difference.

All the examples and case studies in the book come from this research. One of the challenges of writing substantively about real-world diversity is that companies cannot always be forthcoming about their identities, and I have respected that. Therefore, organizations and individuals that have been disguised are marked with asterisks when introduced in the text. All other companies are *not* disguised, and their experiences can be explored further if the reader is interested.

## Searching for the Answers

As I wrote this book, I frequently reflected on my desire to write something that would provide answers to all the burning questions about differences in organizations. I talk with leaders all over the world who earnestly want to know how to deal more productively with differences. I cannot provide all the answers—I don't believe anyone can. But I'm not sure that is such a bad thing. There is something powerful in the collective endeavor of searching for those answers.

It makes sense that no one person can answer these important questions. Really answering them requires that many diverse individuals, holding diverse ideas and perspectives, come together in an empowering context to work in partnership. Their gathering places may be boardrooms or community centers or kitchen tables. They may be discussion boards or chat rooms. Wherever this coming-together happens, that is where the best answers will be found. My hope is that this book can be a resource for anyone engaged in the questioning and the learning.

# 1

# The End of Diversity as We Know It

I met Aaron Evans when I was in Northern California conducting research at Silicon Valley high-tech firms. He struck me as a bright and thoughtful manager, and a genuinely nice guy. His peers had high regard for him, too, as I learned during my visit. As we talked about diversity and its role in his company, he was cordial and a little bit stiff—just his normal demeanor, I assumed. But as we talked, I sensed his increasing agitation. I asked if he was okay. He said he was fine, so we kept talking, but he still seemed uneasy. Finally I inquired, "Aaron, you really seem uncomfortable. Is everything okay?" He sat quietly for a moment and then replied, "To be honest, I know we're supposed to spend this time talking with you about diversity, but I have a real problem with all this. I have an issue with this topic."

From there, we had a long conversation about what was really on his mind. Aaron took great pains to tell me that he was not biased, sexist, racist, or any other such label. Rather, he had a problem with diversity in his company because in the fifteen years he had been a manager there, he had seen diversity efforts do more harm than good. He had felt pressure to hire so-called "diverse" people (code for women and people of color)—who weren't easy to find—when he already had great candidates in his own pipeline who happened to be white males. And then the diverse hires often left the company within two years—or worse, they stayed but just couldn't do the job. Promotion decisions in favor of women and minorities seemed unfair, since people were often pushed forward before they were really ready. He had attended more than a few diversity training programs, but they had had little impact on his day-to-day work. Even worse, the real diversity that mattered to him—how to manage people of diverse styles of thought and work habits—didn't seem to count in the company's definition of diversity.

Eileen Vargas had been working at the same Silicon Valley firm as Aaron Evans for eighteen months. We spoke for a while, and I was struck by her professional, no-nonsense style. She was clearly very smart, both with regard to her particular area of expertise and with regard to the firm's social and political machinations. The more we spoke, the more she seemed to relax, and we began to really talk about her experience there. She described how difficult it had been for her, as a Latina, to fit in. She was clear about the structural impediments: she was only the third female to be hired in her department of thirty-three employees, and the only person of color.

As a seasoned manager, she had known she might have to deal with both unintended and deliberate bias. And she had known she would need to "influence gently" in order to win over skeptical colleagues who would quietly question her credibility when she advocated for cutting-edge ideas. This was all familiar terrain for Eileen.

But she kept feeling that it should be better than this. She had come here because her research had shown that this firm was an industry leader, with senior management who understood the importance of investing in people as a way of creating value. She knew that the CEO had a particular passion for diversity, and she thought that boded well. And even though her department was thin on diversity, in recent years the company as a whole had made great strides in its hiring and promotion of women and people of color.

And she was miserable.

She said to me, "Look, I'm not naive. I know that places like this are almost always difficult for people like me. But it shouldn't be like this. I'm talented and I want to contribute to this company, and there must be a way for me to do that and be properly rewarded for what I offer. I want to work well with my peers and to be a part of this place. I see lots of my colleagues enjoying their work and one another, and I want that, too."

## Current Approaches to Diversity Are Failing

Aaron and Eileen are but two examples of how the admirably passionate pursuit of diversity in organizations has fallen short. Employees, regardless of identity, remain confused, frustrated, and disheartened by the way diversity is managed. Annual reports and websites like Chevron Corporation's boldly proclaim that "having a workforce that reflects the composition of the marketplaces we serve and the communities where we operate is an important competitive advantage."[1] Diversity celebrations abound, with ethnic food days and diversity awareness seminars peppered throughout the year. Companies use such activities to communicate that they are committed to diversity and thriving because of it. In fact, commitment frequently wavers, and more than two decades of research shows that very few organizations are actually thriving because of their diversity.

Greater diversity does not easily translate to greater excellence in performance. It takes work to make that happen. Yet many leaders are content in the illusion that symbolic activities and underfunded training classes will turn their increasingly diverse organizations into world-class performers. It's not that these symbolic activities don't have merit. They often help illuminate the experiences of marginalized and undervalued members of the organization. But they don't make the organization truly more inclusive, and they don't catalyze the performance the organization needs to remain competitive in a dynamic global marketplace.

Most leaders don't doubt the potential of diversity to add value, and they certainly don't intend to disempower and confuse their employees. Yet they do both of these things. And changing that dysfunctionality begins with looking at the facts about the current state of diversity.

### *Increased Diversity Doesn't Always Improve Performance*

Despite assertions that workforce diversity makes an organization better, research says otherwise. A survey of the top research on the connection between diversity and performance over the past decade reveals few reliable studies that show a direct relationship between greater workforce diversity and increased bottom-line performance. Complicated links are much more common. For example, racial diversity neither improves nor diminishes performance in financial services firms, with two exceptions: if the firm is in a strategic growth mode, racial diversity helps. But if it is in a downsizing phase, diversity decreases performance.[2]

In one of the more comprehensive evaluations of the link between diversity and performance, Thomas Kochan and his colleagues examined the impact of race and gender diversity on performance in two information-processing firms, a financial services firm, and a retail company. Across these varied organizations they found little evidence of any direct relationships between increased race and gender diversity in the workforce and higher returns on investment, profits, revenue, costs, or other financial measures.[3]

Indeed, in a large study of fast-food establishments, an even bleaker picture emerged. Joshua Sacco and Neal Schmitt studied the effect of race, age, and gender diversity on the financial performance of more than 3,400 quick-service restaurants. They had hypothesized that diversity would hinder financial performance, reasoning that the disruptions that frequently occur within diverse teams would have a kind of domino effect that would adversely affect financial performance. While their study didn't show that gender or age diversity had any bearing on financial performance, increased racial diversity among employees was correlated with lower levels of profitability.[4]

These results are stark and challenging. It is worth noting, however, that some types of diversity *can* make a positive difference. Specifically, having people with diverse functional backgrounds or tenures on top management teams can positively affect the return on assets.[5] Similarly, racial diversity on boards of directors can increase the return on investment.[6] And managerial diversity may enhance performance for some firms in the long run, if not immediately.[7] These results suggest that increasing diversity *could* affect organizational performance in positive ways. The inquiry must continue. But the unqualified assertion that any kind of diversity will lead to superior performance is just wrong.[8]

### *Diverse Groups Do Perform Better ... Sort Of*

While it's hard to find positive links between diversity and performance for firms, the link between high performance and diversity is clearer with groups or teams. In a survey of team diversity research published in the leading academic journals between 1985 and 2006, one powerful finding stands out: diversity related to work tasks—diversity of functions, expertise, or tenure—leads to better team outcomes.[9]

Teams that include this kind of diversity generate more innovative decisions, consider a wider variety of relevant factors, and engender more thorough debate than groups without it. But it is not all about quality of output. Teams with task-related diversity also generate superior measurable outcomes. For example, a link has been shown between functional diversity and faster time to market for new products in the computer industry.[10] In both quality and quantity of performance, there is undeniable value in having task-related diversity on a team.

But when it comes to diversity of race, gender, and age, the gains in team performance disappear. The same survey of team diversity studies revealed no discernible relationship between these kinds of diversity and team rapport or productivity. Having these demographic diversities may not hurt, but it doesn't make the team function more effectively. In other words, the benefits of demographic diversity commonly suggested in the team performance literature have probably been overstated. Simply increasing the degree of demographic diversity isn't an effective approach for building better teams. Focusing on cultivating task-related diversity is probably the better strategy. The bottom line is that not all diversity is helpful when it comes to making teams more effective.[11]

### *Increased Diversity Doesn't Make Everyone Happier*

Another common hope is that diversity will create a happier, more harmonious workplace. American psychologist Gordon Allport proposed the Contact Hypothesis in 1954, suggesting that people of different groups would generate positive relationships with one another *under the proper conditions.*[12] Many leaders, perhaps forgetting about these conditions—equal group status, common goals, intergroup cooperation, and support from leaders—expect positive effects simply by assembling groups of diverse people. To be more precise, leaders often rely on increased diversity to build commitment, improve motivation, and reduce conflict. Unfortunately, generating more diversity can have the opposite effect on some individuals. One area of research called "relational demography" has focused on how individual employees react to situations in which they work with people who are demographically similar to themselves as opposed to situations in which they work with people who are dissimilar.[13]

This research has shown that working with "dissimilar others" can breed *lower* commitment to the organization, diminish job satisfaction, increase perceptions of discrimination, and generate various other negative attitudes and behaviors. In one study, male managers' commitment to the organization decreased as the number of women in their work units increased. The same thing happened among white managers when people of color increased. Incidentally, in this study, the commitment level for people of color was not affected by the number of whites they worked with. And women were actually *more* committed to the company the more men they were able to work with.[14] So whether a person is a member of the majority or the minority probably influences how he or she feels and acts when entering new diverse situations. Suffice it to say that just putting diverse groups of people together, absent the right context and skills, can create, rather than solve, problems.

### *Hiring for Diversity Is Tough*

Despite the evidence to the contrary, many leaders remain committed to the vision that diversity matters, and they feel accountable for getting people of diverse backgrounds into their organizations. But after two decades of learning about best practices in recruiting and hiring of people who are different, it remains extremely difficult to apply those lessons. According to one survey of more than 2,500 senior HR executives in North America, 29 percent reported that although their managers valued diversity, they didn't know how to recruit people who were different.[15]

Hiring to enhance diversity is difficult because often organizations haven't discovered where to find the talented people they want. Recruiting systems frequently fail to connect hiring managers with the right people. The problem may stem from inadequate access to talent pools of the people who have the desired difference. It's standard practice to seek out these candidates at job fairs or to access culturally specific organizations—the Hispanic Association of Colleges and Universities, for instance, or historically black colleges and universities (HBCUs). But even these sources become overused, and companies may struggle to find candidates to fill their positions.

An additional flaw in many recruiting systems is the fact that job descriptions may not adequately capture real job requirements. Therefore, people who could perform quite well in a job are overlooked because they appear to be unqualified, based on the description. At PWM Group,* a mid-sized private wealth management firm,[16] one managing director reported that he wasn't sure what attributes would lead to high performance in his financial advisor positions, so he had come to rely more heavily on his general sense about who could succeed in the job. He and his firm hadn't done a good job of collecting reliable data on what qualifications correlated with performance.

These recruiting system flaws are exacerbated by the biases that hiring managers invariably hold. A great deal of research outlines the deficiencies of managers in recruiting and hiring people who are different. For example, managers may have stereotyped perceptions about race, age, disabilities, and other differences. Sometimes these biases are conscious and explicit, but perhaps even more damaging are the unconscious and implicit psychological biases that influence decisions about whether to hire an applicant for a position.[17] An especially dramatic example of this phenomenon garnered widespread attention in 2005 when Marianne Bertrand and Sendhil Mullainathan published a study on hiring bias. They had sent fictitious resumes in response to help-wanted ads in Boston and Chicago newspapers, randomly assigning them names that "sounded" African American or white. Resumes with white names received 50 percent more calls for interviews than those with the African American names. This gap was uniform across occupation, industry, and company size.[18]

These dynamics can make it difficult for managers and leaders to hire enough diverse people. Managers I speak with frequently lament that there simply are not enough women or people of color available. And at times this may be true; there may not be a large enough pool of diverse talent for a given position. But more often than not, this perception is fueled more by poor recruiting systems and biases than by reality. The challenge is to establish the conditions for transforming that perception into energetic and innovative thinking about how to find the people you need, no matter what.

***Retaining a Diverse Workforce Is Tough***

Hiring is only part of the headache that leaders face as they attempt to build more diverse organizations. Attrition statistics show that there is still that all-too-familiar revolving door for many women and people of color: they are hired but leave more quickly than their white male peers. Losing any employee is costly, but losing employees who contribute to diversity goals takes a huge toll on companies that are trying to build and sustain a diverse workforce. Often they have made extra investments to attract these individuals—investments that are lost when people leave prematurely. And retention rates are generally lower for women and people of color relative to white and male employees.[19] Moreover, annual voluntary turnover is nearly 30 percent higher among people of color.[20]

The causes are varied. In a large study of black, Hispanic, and Native American managers, the subjects reported that their willingness to remain in a company was influenced by several important factors. First they looked for access to developmental opportunities that would prepare them to advance in the organization. This is a common finding: people want a chance to learn, grow, and be rewarded for their efforts. In addition, these managers sought timely and accurate performance feedback. Supervisors are sometimes reluctant—especially in U.S. organizations—to provide concise negative feedback to employees of color. They fear that a bias complaint may be lodged against them and that such a complaint, valid or not, could damage their reputation and their career. As a result, managers of color often are deprived of the information they need to improve. They are blindsided when they finally do get feedback, because often by that point the problem has gotten worse. Managers in the study reported that access to real-time feedback was critical. They also said that a firm's active commitment to diversity was a positive motivation for staying. At the same time, they were watchful of how the firm managed perceptions of bias or discrimination. When it was proactive, they were much more likely to stay in the organization.[21]

Adding to the challenges of maintaining a diverse workforce is the fact that when women or people of color join work groups, white men who are in those groups become flight risks. One set of studies examined organizational attachment—how much a person feels committed to staying at an organization—in diverse working groups. The researchers discovered that having women and people of color join predominantly white male workgroups lowered the attachment levels for the white men in those groups. That lower level of attachment translated into a greater likelihood of leaving the organization.[22] This suggests that the retention dilemma is multifaceted: people who typically increase diversity are at risk to leave at a greater rate than their white male counterparts, but if they stay, the white men are more likely to leave. When all is said and done, these dynamics can make it difficult to maintain a diverse workforce.

### *Resistance to Diversity Is Alive and Well*

In addition to the challenges of finding and retaining diverse employees, leaders seeking to promote diversity continue to face fierce resistance. The first line of resistance comes from those who feel the greatest threat of losing the comfort and status they experience with the existing workforce structure. In the U.S. context, this typically means whites, males, heterosexuals, U.S. citizens, or any combination of those. The labels may be different in other countries, but the key characteristic is that these people belong to mainstream or dominant groups. Resistance may take the form of hostile and aggressive behavior or it may take more subtle forms, such as refusal to engage with or active ostracism of "different" colleagues.

At an institutional level, resistance manifests itself in discriminatory behavior in which dominant group members implement and support practices that disadvantage diverse colleagues. At one of the regional field offices of PWM Group, it was common practice to limit the territories of junior associates. On average, men in the organization had longer tenure than women—the company had only recently made concerted efforts to bring women into the sales force, which explains why women had shorter tenures. As a result, women had less desirable territories than their male counterparts and were unable to move product as effectively as the men. As a result, they received less favorable evaluations, and some were eventually dismissed for poor performance.

No one in management intended to create a disadvantage for the women—not only would that have been illegal, it would clearly not have been in the company's best interest. In speaking with the sales and marketing executives, I found them genuinely surprised, concerned, and trying to understand what had created the situation. They ultimately decided to change the territory allocation process, though some performance differences between men and women persisted.

This example captures the subtle impact of institutional resistance. Practices that were developed and implemented without any intentional bias continue to be effective for a time. Then the workforce becomes more diverse, and those procedures are disadvantageous for people who are different. But it is difficult to change them, in part because they are so common that it's hard to identify them as the source of the problem. In the same way that we rarely analyze the act of breathing, employees rarely question the viability of such practices: "It's just how we do things." Moreover, employees from the dominant majority, who are accustomed to successfully using these practices, bristle at the accusation that they are flawed.

Resistance can take unexpected forms. Sometimes people who are different react negatively to diversity initiatives. They may feel "spotlighted" and experience undue performance pressure as a result, which can increase stress and actually reduce performance. Rather than confront such challenges, people who are different may resist being associated with anything related to their identity group, or to diversity as a whole.

One of the enduring observations shared by people who aren't part of the majority is that sometimes individuals from their own minority group are their harshest workplace critics. One example is the so-called "Queen Bee Syndrome," in which established female managers in predominantly male organizations fail to support junior female colleagues.[23] When people who are different undermine one another, they provide further justification for those who resist greater diversity. The heterosexual manager who encounters a gay colleague criticizing another gay employee may feel less dissonance in then criticizing or stereotyping gay employees as a group. This can quickly turn into overt or subtle discrimination that prevents talented gay colleagues from succeeding in the organization.

### *We Can't Seem to Learn*

For corporate stakeholders who really want change that takes advantage of diversity, what's especially discouraging is that the vehicles for learning how to do so are typically ineffective. Alexandra Kalev, Frank Dobbin, and Erin Kelly examined the effectiveness of various diversity activities in 708 private-sector establishments from 1971 to 2002. They made some surprising discoveries. For example, attempts to counteract managerial bias by providing evaluative feedback typically had no effect on changing the manager's attitudes or behavior. And diversity training had virtually no effect on changing behavior, frequently generating backlash instead.[24]

For years, efforts to change companies' demographics to make them more competitive have focused on bringing people from diverse backgrounds into companies and helping them thrive there. Yet executives and managers continue to feel that their goals are unrealized. There is a particular frustration associated with trying to move the diversity needle: many leaders observe that they have been undertaking the accepted best practices for years, but getting very little *sustained* change. This frustrating situation has produced skepticism about the effectiveness of diversity initiatives of any kind. And it has reinforced deep-seated mistrust between diverse members within an organization.

Perhaps the greatest cost of this wheel-spinning is that the potential advantages of diversity remain largely unrealized. What makes it so difficult for so many companies to gain traction when they attempt to create greater diversity? Why do so many leaders and managers feel frustrated? Why are current approaches to diversity failing?

## The Problem with Managing Diversity

Don't let the portrait I've painted obscure the positive results that diversity, once catalyzed, can produce. Diversity *can* increase sales performance. Focusing on targeted types of diversity can enhance productivity, widen the pool of talent flowing into an organization, open up new markets, and increase overall organizational effectiveness.[25] Diversity in groups can foster cohesiveness and teamwork, improve communication, accelerate decision-making, and generate innovation and creativity.[26]

Yet in many organizations these benefits of diversity are not being realized, and research helps us understand some of the reasons why. For example, diverse groups that perform effectively tend to handle conflict early in the group's formation by channeling it toward accomplishing the task, not toward group members. Interpersonal conflicts will pop up within any group, especially one whose members have diverse backgrounds and divergent views. But high-performing diverse groups perform well because they practice disagreeing about task-related issues before they disagree about personal issues.[27]

But there are larger reasons for the failure of traditional diversity approaches. Throughout this book, I'll refer to these traditional approaches as "Managing Diversity" approaches. Managing Diversity describes a set of difference-related activities practiced in most U.S. organizations. These activities are readily adopted and, when well executed, are considered best practice. A number of resources such as corporate benchmark reports and analyses of diversity management approaches converge on the set of Managing Diversity practices and activities that includes the following:

- Ensuring senior leadership commitment
- Articulating a business-case rationale
- Creating an office of diversity staffed by a senior or chief diversity officer
- Establishing a diversity council of select "diverse" employees from throughout the organization, along with a small number of senior white male managers or executives
- Establishing employee resource groups (also called affinity or network groups) based on demographic identities such as race, gender, and sexual orientation
- Focusing on the recruitment and hiring of women and people of color
- Promoting the advancement and retention of minorities using both mentoring programs and sponsorship programs
- Sponsoring ongoing diversity training
- Engaging in targeted marketing to recruit certain groups
- Creating relationships with community organizations that represent target groups

This list is comprehensive but not exhaustive; other activities may belong on it. And none of these is necessarily negative—all of them were good ideas at one point or another. But they haven't been able to fundamentally transform most of the organizations that have adopted them. Here is why.

### *How Managing Diversity Can Limit People of Difference*

One of the primary intents of the Managing Diversity programs has been to promote the successful integration of people who have traditionally been marginalized in most organizations. The ultimate goal is to have these people channel their talents and efforts toward the objectives of the organization. But paradoxically, Managing Diversity programs can hinder rather than facilitate attainment of this goal. One example of this paradox is the incentive that rewards managers for hiring and retaining women or persons of color in their departments. Managers receive rewards (or avoid penalties) if they maintain a head count that demonstrates departmental diversity. This can certainly motivate a manager to make that critical hire. But it can also have the unintended consequence of motivating managers to prevent an employee from advancing and moving elsewhere in the company.

At Worldview Studios,* a large multimedia entertainment company, an African American woman named Jolene had been heavily recruited. After nearly two years in the same position, she couldn't understand why she hadn't been promoted. Her performance reviews were consistently strong, and she seemed to have a good rapport with her manager and her colleagues. But she realized that she was one of very few women of color in the company and the only one in her department, and as accountability for creating diversity spread through the company, she had become a prized commodity. The diversity-driven incentive structure motivated her manager to keep her in his department as long as possible. Each of her performance reviews included subtle areas for improvement that justified withholding a promotion. Jolene was as talented as ever, but her performance degraded as she learned that no matter how well she did, she wouldn't be promoted.

A similar dynamic prevents people who are different from moving laterally. An episode of the popular science fiction television series *Star Trek: The Next Generation* portrayed the dilemma. The U.S.S. *Enterprise*, the flagship space vessel of an organization known as the United Federation of Planets, had been dispatched to take command of several other ships before an upcoming conflict. Each *Enterprise* officer was assigned to command a ship—except for the android Commander Data, a sophisticated robot with human form. When he inquired dispassionately about this exclusion (he lacked emotional awareness, so he was exceedingly rational), his captain realized there was no reason not to assign him to a ship. But when Data assumed command, his first officer asked to be reassigned. He didn't believe an android was capable of commanding a starship.

This science fiction scenario exemplifies the "role-slotting" that occurs in organizations.[28] By virtue of their novelty, "different" people are often misjudged on their competency, thanks to widely held stereotypes about their capabilities. The Japanese are engineers, women are HR professionals, and Australians are social directors. Such stereotypes shape perceptions of the abilities of anyone who is different. They also shape perceptions of what people cannot do. Superiors and colleagues come to see them as competent only in a particular area, even though they may have a tremendous breadth of abilities. And, as was the case for Jolene, the persistent feedback that she couldn't perform in a different capacity ultimately became a self-fulfilling prophecy.

When people in an organization hold stereotyped views about particular groups, Managing Diversity initiatives can inadvertently feed career-limiting behavior by highlighting individuals' membership in those groups.

Mr. Data the android, by the way, turned out to be a decisive and clever commanding officer, much to the surprise of his subordinates.

### *Managing Diversity Stifles Collaboration*

The foundation of Managing Diversity activity came largely from the imperative to counter discrimination and mistreatment based on identity differences like race and gender. In the United States, this is backed by the force of law: legal mandates set the stage for traditional diversity activity. The Civil Rights Act of 1964 prohibits discrimination by employers covered under the law on the basis of race, color, religion, sex, or national origin. It also prohibits discrimination against anyone because of his or her association with another individual of a particular race, color, religion, sex, or national origin. An employer cannot discriminate against someone because of an interracial marriage, for instance.[29]

But this legal legacy has begun to undermine the aspirational goals of diversity work—to support people of many different perspectives and backgrounds in working and living together in generative ways. The intent to abide by the law to reduce the risk of legal liability has had the unintended effect of encouraging people to reduce risk in their relationships with people who are different, especially those from legally protected classes. This manifests itself in many ways: not talking with others about controversial topics, not providing constructive feedback, and simply not interacting in any way. Productivity and innovation suffer severely in a culture of caution.

In discussing a discrimination lawsuit against his professional services firm, one corporate lawyer commented that the firm wasn't being sued because someone had said something inappropriate. Of course, that does happen and must be dealt with. But, he said, they were being sued because no one said anything.[30] His point was that the norm of carefulness that encouraged managers not to engage with members of the group that had filed the lawsuit had left those individuals out of the loop in critical discussions, limited their access to necessary feedback, and left them with increasingly impoverished work relationships that made it impossible for them to be successful. They felt that their only reasonable options were to leave the company or to file a lawsuit.

Managing Diversity approaches have inadvertently left leaders, managers, and their organizations in the difficult position of needing to create change while not being able to talk openly about how to do so.

### *Managing Diversity Wasn't Designed for Long-Term Change*

Managing Diversity activity was always built for the short run. It is triage work. You see a demographic crisis in workforce makeup (a crisis that was and continues to be heightened by rapid demographic shifts in the labor market) and you respond by identifying steps that will head off that crisis. That's what targeted recruiting and hiring and quotas are all about. But now we find ourselves living in a complex global economy in which coming up with sustainable solutions, not just temporary fixes, is what's needed. You can't follow the Managing Diversity tactic of ratcheting up recruitment of "diverse" people without solving the problem of why those same people continue to leave more frequently than their majority counterparts. "Let's get people in the door and see what happens" is just not good enough anymore. Managing Diversity efforts are thus often unsustainable; they don't really create the kind of change that businesses and society need to remain economically competitive and socially just.

Most companies and leaders who are genuinely engaged in diversity work are looking for sustainable improvement in firm performance. But that consistent, long-term change in the way business is done is likely to be elusive if their efforts remain grounded in traditional diversity practices. First of all, Managing Diversity is, at its core, crisis-driven. Many companies have undertaken diversity work either in anticipation of or in reaction to external pressures such as discrimination litigation. David Pitts and his colleagues found as much when they surveyed a representative sample of organizations that were engaged in traditional diversity efforts. In an effort to understand whether the work was motivated by external pressures likely to precipitate crises, they found that such pressures were, in fact, among the strongest drivers for Managing Diversity programs.[31]

A hallmark of traditional diversity work is that it is "add-on" activity—tactical work that people undertake in addition to their regular jobs. So it isn't surprising that it takes an urgent situation to mobilize action. This is exactly why traditional diversity is so frequently crisis-driven. That crisis may be acute ("We're being sued!") or chronic ("We have to hurry to stay ahead of demographic changes!"). Either way, operating in crisis mode encourages tactical actions that often lead to short-lived changes.

Furthermore, traditional diversity approaches typically promote a menu of metrics and incentives designed to generate visible and timely results. But the unintended consequence is that diversity stakeholders are motivated to keep producing "quick-win" approaches that perpetuate short-term change without requiring long-term transformation. For example, the impetus to implement a diversity initiative (created by the crisis of a lawsuit) prompted FedTech Technologies,* a computer manufacturing company, to establish an incentive for hiring persons of color. If managers failed to do so, their year-end bonuses suffered (in fact, the company had created a disincentive to lead a team without anyone of color on it).

As a result, managers rabidly sought out candidates and began to hire them. Within eighteen months of the mandate, representation of managers of color had increased. However, those managers were disproportionately represented in the lower ratings of performance, making them more vulnerable to turnover.

Similarly, Aeolian Accounting* faced a serious dilemma in 1997. For years the small auditing firm had lagged behind competitors in advancing women into partnership positions. Its pipeline was anemic, as it had relatively few women associates in the firm. The unspoken rationale had been that since it was lean, it couldn't afford to make "mistakes" in hiring, so it had followed a conservative strategy of hiring from familiar pools of talent. The result was that the vast majority of associates were men. In a bold move, CEO Alan Jerrold* declared that for the coming fiscal year, only women associate hires would be approved. Jerrold was pleased that six women joined the firm that year, compared to only one the previous two years combined. But when he took stock of the situation in 2008, he was discouraged. By this time many of the women who had entered in 1997 should have become partners. But none of them had been promoted to partner.

The cases of FedTech and Aeolian are similar in two ways. In the first place, both organizations implemented a hiring initiative based primarily on a demographic characteristic. Both initiatives were driven by the organization's anxiety over a diversity crisis. Second, managers were given the directive to hire people of color and women with no guidance on how to create an environment in which they could be successful. The resulting demographic disparities had occurred because of the exclusionary nature of the organizations' culture and practices. It made little sense to bring in members of groups who had traditionally struggled in that culture and expect them *not* to face the same challenges in that same culture.

Traditional diversity relies heavily on relatively simple measures such as an organization's current demographic profile and how it has evolved over time, specifically data related to recruiting (who was interviewed, who was hired), promotions (who was considered, who was promoted), and retention (who left the organization, how turnover rates compare across demographic groups). The other common approach is to use employee opinion data as a way to evaluate the effectiveness of a diversity initiative. Surveys, focus groups, and exit interviews can be used to monitor more subtle and systemic aspects—organizational culture, for instance, and barriers such as lack of mentoring programs and exclusion from informal networking groups.[32]

The question is whether these metrics do an adequate job of measuring what matters most in generating long-term change. How will the head count of people with different demographic characteristics really help an organization create sustainable change? How will attitudinal surveys support the behavioral changes that would make a difference? These questions must be answered if long-term sustained change is the goal.

### *Managing Diversity Hasn't Provided Answers to Legitimate Pushback*

Managing Diversity efforts are fundamentally change efforts. Most initiatives try to capitalize on the differences among employees, customers, suppliers, and/or external stakeholders as a way to generate greater organizational performance. But one of the criteria for judging whether a change effort is effective is how it manages the resistance that inevitably arises. The Achilles' heel of the argument for diversity has been that greater diversity doesn't guarantee superior bottom-line performance.[33] Diversity proponents have tended to worry that this is a fatal flaw in making their case. Critics might ask, from a purely utilitarian perspective, "What is the point of generating more diversity if, in fact, it won't improve performance, or could diminish performance?" Traditional diversity initiatives, as a result, are sometimes characterized by a kind of fragility. Proponents struggle to reinforce the legitimacy of diversity efforts in the face of skeptics and resisters. And repeatedly being questioned about the importance of diversity activity can create a defensive posture.

In light of this, one of the most significant challenges for diversity professionals is dealing with the pushback on diversity activity from members of the organization who support the status quo. In a Managing Diversity world, diversity professionals and advocates take comfort in the fact that this is a manifestation of resistance to change. And it surely is. But just because resisters are making their points just to be oppositional doesn't mean those points aren't legitimate.

When a critic asks why the female employee with lower qualifications was hired over the male employee, most Managing Diversity scripts don't equip proponents very well to answer, "Because we want more women. Period." In response to the observation that matching company demographics to society demographics is arbitrary, it can be a challenge to admit, "You're right, it is. We shouldn't be pursuing that aggressive a demographic shift." Or to say, "We should pursue a much more aggressive demographic shift." As with any change initiative, Managing Diversity rationales are imperfect and embody contradictions. Flaws will constantly be pointed out by those resistant to diversity. Imperfections and contradictions are not fatal flaws per se. Failing to address them adequately is. That is one of the problems with Managing Diversity.

There are a number of thoughtful responses to the critically important question of why organizations should undertake diversity, some of which I will address in this book. Some of them are complex, and that complexity will make it easier for those who resist diversity to dismiss or undermine it. But there is no reason that leaders who advocate for change can't respond to that resistance with compelling alternatives. Hopefully, some will be found in these pages.

### *Managing Diversity Has Lost the Attention of Many Stakeholders*

When I am invited to speak about diversity, the feedback I often receive in advance is that the audience is looking for "something new" about diversity because many of the conventional messages are well worn. Numerous writers in the academic and popular press have noted the prevalence of diversity fatigue as a hindrance to achieving significant change in organizations.[34] What is noteworthy is that this apathy isn't simply an issue of resistance, of status quo supporters refusing to change. This disengagement affects critics and supporters alike. Critics disengage as a way to express their dissatisfaction that Managing Diversity continues to operate without making concessions to the criticisms leveled against it. Supporters disengage because Managing Diversity either hasn't produced results or the results it has produced haven't been sustained. As a result, these proponents—especially those who are themselves different from the norm—feel disappointed and discouraged.

## How Can It Be Done Differently?

Managing Diversity has been an appropriate and necessary step in the evolution of how organizations engage difference. And despite its shortcomings, it has profoundly changed the thoughts, feelings, and actions of people at all levels in many organizations. To construe this discussion and what follows as a repudiation of Managing Diversity thus misses the mark. Though some might debate it, Managing Diversity efforts, when executed ably, were bold, innovative, and right for the time. It's just that times are changing and a fresh approach that builds on Managing Diversity is needed.

The purpose of this book is to stimulate thinking about an alternative way of making diversity work that addresses the challenges presented by Managing Diversity. This alternative approach makes diversity a core part of the strategic capability of an organization. It engages employees, customers, suppliers, and external stakeholders in a collaborative effort to make the organization more successful and more resilient. This new approach to diversity is one that can transform the way an organization operates, grows, and thrives. This alternative is Leveraging Difference.

## Key Takeaways

1. Traditional approaches to managing differences in organizations—Managing Diversity approaches—are less and less effective in our new global marketplace.
2. Having greater diversity in an organization doesn't always translate into superior outcomes.
3. Benefits of diversity are easier to see when looking at team performance, but only for certain kinds of differences. Diver-

sity related to work tasks—diversity of functions, expertise, or tenure—leads to greater team productivity and stronger rapport than do diversity of race, gender, and age.

4. People don't automatically like working together when they feel divided by difference. Introducing some kinds of diversity can diminish commitment and increase turnover.
5. Hiring for diversity is difficult because organizations don't look in the right places, the jobs they are recruiting for aren't always well defined, and even if job responsibilities are clear and the right people are available, biases can prevent managers from hiring them.
6. Retaining people who are different is challenging, because organizational cultures and practices aren't always designed to support them, and because majority employees—white men, in the U.S.-focused studies we surveyed—aren't always comfortable in more diverse settings.
7. Resistance persists, and learning about difference suffers because of it.
8. Managing Diversity approaches haven't succeeded in delivering better outcomes for a number of reasons:

    - They can limit the very people they are designed to help by spotlighting them and making them the focus of stereotyping and role-slotting.
    - Fear about fully engaging difference stifles collaboration and keeps people from building effective working relationships.
    - Managing Diversity activities aren't well suited to effect long-term change, promoting "quick-win" approaches that lead to short-term change without ongoing transformation.

9. Managing Diversity approaches often do not effectively counter resistance. They have lost the attention of both advocates and detractors, discouraging people of difference and making diversity seem less relevant as an organizational issue.

# 2

# The Beginning of Leveraging Difference

I was working with a team of executives from a Fortune 100 company, helping them to increase the numbers of African American and women managers. I had just finished a particularly lively meeting with the chief operating officer and some of his direct reports. I was feeling pretty energized by their commitment to the work, and I felt I could help them with their efforts. During the break, the COO approached me to chat about a variety of things—our families and our professional histories, including my experience helping companies like his navigate through tricky issues like diversity. We talked a bit about some of the current strategic challenges for the company, and I sensed he was pleasantly surprised that we could have an engaged conversation about strategy, operational efficiency, and supply-chain frustrations—I don't think he expected that at a diversity program. Since our first meeting four weeks before this, we had been building a nice rapport together.

After several minutes of conversation he said, "Okay, let me ask you a question. And this is a question I won't ask in the room." Of course, I was intrigued. He went on, "Let's say you help us to really get some traction and we are able to up our numbers of women and African Americans. That would constitute a success, right?"

I wasn't sure where this was going, but I played along. "Definitely," I said.

"Yeah," he shot back. "So what?"

He had caught me off balance. I had assumed it would be obvious to someone like him. "Look," he continued, "I have a lot of confidence that we can make some of these talent management changes. Our HR folks are top-notch and I can see this working—we will get more qualified African Americans and women to join this company. But how is this really going to make a difference for this business, above and beyond the PR? We can get all the different colors of the rainbow at the table, but what difference will it *really* make?"

This COO was thoughtful on issues of diversity, and he genuinely wanted to understand how to take advantage of diversity for his company. He needed an answer that would both help him recommit to the importance of diversity and help him credibly lead his people in developing and committing to practices that would sustain diversity in the organization. He needed a new framing for diversity. He needed to learn about Leveraging Difference.

## After Managing Diversity

Business bookshelves and academic journals are replete with titles about how to "manage diversity," as though the inevitable reality is that once you put different people and perspectives together, anarchy will ensue and the chaos that develops will have to be managed! In fairness, all of us can probably remember being put together with someone quite different from us and experiencing some disruption as a result. But there are also numerous examples of differences creating synergy and harmony. What if the most important leadership activity was actually to *catalyze* diversity, not just manage it? This question is at the core of the distinction between traditional Managing Diversity and the new Leveraging Difference. Table 1 offers a more refined picture of what distinguishes the two ways of looking at diversity.

**Table 1 Managing Diversity versus Leveraging Difference**

| | **Managing Diversity** | **Leveraging Difference** |
|---|---|---|
| Context | Embedded in U.S. cultural and business context | Applicable to multiple cultural and business contexts |
| Leadership Perspective | Diversity is a problem to be solved | Difference is an opportunity to be seized |
| Strategic Focus | • Emphasis on HR management to drive activity related to differences<br>• Diversity activity linked to short-term results | • Emphasis on enterprise strategy to drive outcomes related to difference<br>• Diversity activity linked to short- and long-term results<br>• Focus on building strategic capability for leveraging difference |
| Scope of Difference Engaged | Narrow set of differences are relevant | Broader scope of differences are relevant |
| Impact of Change Processes | • Learning for some individuals<br>• Increase in representation of targeted differences<br>• Higher overall levels of resistance to diversity change | • Learning for broader set of individuals<br>• Increase in representation of strategically relevant differences<br>• Lower levels of overall resistance to difference-based change<br>• Organization positioned to leverage other differences in the future |

For the purpose of clarity, the discussion that follows highlights the extreme characteristics of each frame. In reality, leaders and organizations may incorporate qualities from both frames, using one or the other in various arenas of organizational life. For example, an organization might use a Leveraging Difference frame in relation to customers while using the Managing Diversity frame in its talent management. But knowing the differences between the two frames is essential for understanding when one frame or the other is operating. The distinction also helps leaders understand how shifting from Managing Diversity to Leveraging Difference can create value.

## What's the Context?

Activities in organizations operate within given social, historical, and political contexts. The Managing Diversity frame can be described as an especially U.S. approach to difference. A great deal of the emphasis and philosophy behind Managing Diversity flows from the social, historical, and political backdrop of intergroup dynamics in the United States. For example, race as defined in the U.S. is a socially constructed concept, as opposed to a biological one.[1] In the U.S., I define myself—and am typically defined by others—as black or African American because of my skin color, my facial features, and so on. However, my lineage also contains European (Scottish) and American Indian (Cherokee) ancestry. Like many other African Americans, I have tended to deemphasize these other parts of my cultural identity because black racial identity is so much more salient for people with my color and features. This can be true for people of other racial groups as well. It's as though, for any culture, there are racial "folders" with labels defined by history, social policy, politics, and habit. We learn to place ourselves—and others—into the folders that best describe us, even if our identities really are much more complex. And we rarely allow anyone to be in more than one folder.

When it comes to race, the Managing Diversity frame has relied on a set of folders labeled black/African American, white/Caucasian, Asian/Pacific Islander, Hispanic, and Native American. The folder metaphor may extend to other kinds of differences as well. The point is that every national culture has its unique set of folders, and Managing Diversity and its folders are firmly embedded in the United States.

In contrast, the Leveraging Difference model is not embedded solely in U.S. context. Any organization in any country can adopt this approach as a way of improving how it operates. For example, in Vietnam a small sample of business leaders queried about the value of diversity responded that the Managing Diversity model wasn't useful to them. They reported that the Vietnamese don't struggle with racial issues in the way they are defined in the United States. Skin-color differences are less pronounced. Gender inequities are evident, but interest in gender dynamics varies.

However, there *are* diversity tensions in Vietnam. Significant and enduring social and economic disparities exist among the fifty-four ethnic groups within the country. The ethnic majority groups, the Kinh and the Hoa, have substantially higher living standards than the "minority" households from the other ethnic groups. Some groups seem to be doing well as the result of assimilating with the Kinh-Hoa majority economically and culturally. Others are attempting to integrate economically while retaining distinct cultural identities. Another group, the Central Highland Minorities, is being left behind in the growth process.[2] These ethnic group differences invariably affect access to talent pools and networks in Vietnamese organizations (and in global organizations operating in Vietnam). This, in turn, affects the ability to leverage cultural, ethnic, and regional differences.

## Leadership Perspective

Difference-based change happens only in the presence of leadership commitment to that change. The kind of change that unfolds depends upon that leader's mindset toward diversity and difference. The two frames are associated with two distinct leadership mindsets. The Managing Diversity frame is typically enacted by leaders who have a *problem*-focused mindset toward difference. In contrast, leaders in a Leveraging Difference frame are usually focused on the *opportunities* the difference creates.

Ryan and Robert Quinn, in their book *Lift*,[3] develop the notion of comfort-centered approaches to situations, distinct from purpose-centered approaches. They argue that when people operate from a comfort-centered stance, they often approach situations as problems and seek to solve them. While there is nothing especially wrong with this—many problems do need solving—it contrasts with a more powerful alternative approach. Being purpose-centered usually expands the options for dealing with a situation and helps create previously unimagined and effective outcomes.

By the same token, leaders operating from a Managing Diversity viewpoint have difficulty seeing difference and diversity as anything but a problem when faced with the need to execute on diversity activities. They often understand the benefits of diversity in the abstract. But they struggle to understand how to turn diversity into an advantage in day-to-day situations. Since they don't see the practical benefit of diversity, they experience it as a burden and sometimes even a threat.

One manager from Home Building, Inc.,* a mid-sized construction company, lamented that diversity in his company was all about head count and he was frustrated because he understood neither why it was important nor how he could "find the heads." For the Managing Diversity leader, diversity frequently goes hand in hand with stress. For leaders who share group identity with the majority of their employees (for example, white male leaders in a white male organization), diversity can generate psychological dissonance ("I'm not fully committed, but I have to act like I am") and disrupt common routines ("It's hard enough to hire; now I have to find diverse candidate slates, too?"). In contrast, a leader whose group identity differs from that of most employees may experience different stresses. A woman leading a predominantly male organization may feel pressure to make sure she doesn't appear to favor women. Therefore she may feel that her commitment to diversity activities is in conflict with her need to seem objective and fair.

The stress that flows from these diversity pressures creates another challenging by-product: threat rigidity. When people experience stress and disruption, they think, feel, and act in more constrained ways. They are less open to new information or novel ways of thinking about an issue. They are more likely to rely on well-learned or habitual behaviors. This makes it all the more difficult to see diversity as an opportunity.[4] When I'm working with a group of leaders, I often ask the participants how they felt when they heard they were coming to a session on diversity. The response is almost always underwhelming. This lack of excitement and energy is symptomatic of a Managing Diversity frame. The problem-focused mentality inherent in Managing Diversity is frequently de-energizing for leaders.

In contrast, the Leveraging Difference frame invites leaders to explore the opportunities inherent when diversity of thought, identity, and perspective are present. This focus on opportunity is expansive and energizing. Recent research has shown the benefits of energized engagement on both performance and relationships in work settings. The physiological stimulation experienced by an individual in this state facilitates cognitive clarity and focus. This has the effect of energizing others with whom that person is working, stimulating more complex and innovative thinking, attracting and creating tangible resources to address the issues at hand, and generating higher levels of measurable performance. Interestingly, this sort of highly engaged performance feeds a cycle of success: high performance legitimizes the work being undertaken by the leader or team, and that supports ongoing efficacy and continued high performance.[5]

At The Fashion Place Company,* a well-known retail company, a senior leader named Hal became committed to engaging difference because of his experience collaborating with a female colleague, Olivia. This woman had the reputation of being quiet and having little to offer in the way of innovative ideas. But as Hal built a good working relationship with Olivia, he found her to be pretty quirky; she was a highly associative thinker, and it was often hard to have a linear conversation with her because she kept interjecting some new and seemingly unrelated thought. Over time, Hal realized that Olivia was one of the most creative thinkers he had ever met when it came to marketing. Together they cultivated a new—and very successful—line of children's outerwear. Hal became a champion for individuals who operated differently from the norm. In search of outcomes like his and Olivia's, he committed to interacting with colleagues who didn't always fit in with the crowd. Not all of these collaborations were successful, but he persevered, realizing that at any point he might tap into benefits from people who didn't quite fit.[6]

Leaders operating from a Managing Diversity frame are stuck in a self-limiting mindset. To them, differences among employees create problems that must be solved. Leaders in a Leveraging Difference frame explore and exploit the conflicts that arise from difference, rather than squelching them, because they know that in discomfort and disagreement lie opportunities for innovation.

When Felton Barnes was promoted to general manager of the highest-performing business unit at Delvin Mining Corporation,* he restructured his division's leadership team. He replaced five members of the team (all senior white men with long histories in the division) with individuals who had different functional backgrounds and more experience in other divisions. Four of the five were African American and three were women. He made the changes because he believed his predecessor had been reluctant to focus on continuous improvement in the manufacturing process, and he worried that the old team would share that conservatism.

The division's sole product was also the company's top-selling product, so it was understandable that the old regime would be reluctant to fix what wasn't broken. But Barnes believed he could improve sales. This would require converting to a more efficient manufacturing process, but he was committed to the change.

Barnes worked rigorously to build his team into a high-functioning unit. For nearly two years, he enlisted the help of consultants skilled in working with diverse leadership teams. He and his team built knowledge about their collective functional competencies, learned how to engage in dialogue that encouraged creative thinking, and learned to negotiate cultural and gender differences among themselves. Team members reported measurable increases in interpersonal trust as well as in their trust of the competencies of their teammates. Barnes also utilized a personal coach to help him be more inspirational and less defensive when faced with resistance. As a result of the team's leadership, new processes were implemented that resulted in two consecutive years of sales increases and record-setting profit.[7]

## Strategic Focus

Perhaps the central difference between the two approaches is in strategic focus. Simply put, Managing Diversity places the focus primarily on managing human resources in the organization. Managing Diversity initiatives are deeply rooted in attempts to "put the right people on the bus" at all levels of the organization, as well as to insure that the organization is operating fairly and equitably with regard to employees. With Leveraging Difference, firms focus on encouraging sustainable competitive advantage in broader ways. This includes the HR focus and talent management highlighted in the Managing Diversity frame, but it also explores how differences might be integral to the activities that build sustainable competitive advantage: marketing to globally diverse customers, designing more innovative and effective operational processes, and even managing mergers, acquisitions, and interfirm alliances.

The Managing Diversity strategic focus is clearly illustrated by AMEXCO Corp.* This company had the reputation for being an industry leader in diversity and inclusion (D&I). The CEO was passionate about the importance of diversity and tasked his senior HR leader to "make diversity work for us." The HR leader took this mandate seriously and conducted an audit of the diversity activities in place in the organization, including three different training programs in three separate divisions. The remaining four divisions had no diversity training activities in place. The HR leader proceeded to hire a director of diversity from an internal pool of candidates—an African American engineer who had been with the company for twelve years and had a modestly successful performance record. He was universally praised as competent, collaborative, and affable. Moreover, he was well respected among employees of color. He accepted the position with the understanding that he would serve for two years and then return to his previous function. The idea was that the position would include career development elements—greater visibility with other divisions in the company, for instance.

As director of diversity, he was responsible for coordinating diversity activities as well as generating and carrying out a diversity strategy. The director focused on 1) articulating a business case for diversity in the company; 2) setting recruiting targets for people of color; 3) setting promotion targets for greater representation at higher levels; and 4) beginning mandatory standardized diversity training for all company divisions. The HR leader was pleased with this approach and eager to share this information with the CEO.

This is a familiar story in many Fortune 500 companies. And it captures three core characteristics of the strategic approach that flows from a Managing Diversity frame. First, diversity always resides within or somewhere near the human resource function. Often the diversity function rests within HR and the dedicated diversity professional reports to HR leadership. The problem is that this predisposes everyone to assume that diversity is purely an HR issue and keeps them from seeing other strategic benefits that could result from focusing on difference. It also places diversity efforts in a staff-focused arena that is marginalized in many organizations. Most AMEXCO employees thought of HR as an important function, but one that was, as one manager put it, a "service" function, one not seen as central to the business, regardless of its actual strategic importance. HR professionals were seen as consultants within the organization, and in AMEXCO many were not well respected. By association, diversity activity was seen as tangential to the business. At best, it was a laudable activity if there was time for it, at worst an excuse to implement unfair employment practices and reverse discrimination.

Second, AMEXCO's diversity activities tended to be tactical in nature, linked to results that would be visible in the short run. Critical activities such as setting recruiting targets were undertaken without carefully considering the strategic importance of talent acquisition. Setting targets is a logical way to bring in more diverse people. But AMEXCO hadn't done a good job of examining what value was created by increasing its representation of these candidates. So recruiting was undertaken without a clear and compelling strategic reason for doing it—except that the CEO was passionate about diversity and wanted to see "results."

Third, all of the activities undertaken by the director focused on short-term results. Targets for recruiting and promotion could be measured quickly and easily. Diversity training could be implemented and evaluations collected at each offering. These activities produced visible results quickly. Moreover, the director was motivated to generate these quick wins, because he was to be in the position for a finite term and wanted to have something to show for his efforts. As a result, no one was responsible for focusing on the longer-term, more intractable challenge of having a workforce with greater diversity in demographics, skills, or experience.

Contrast the AMEXCO experience with that of New Frontiers Financial Services, Inc.,* a wealth management firm that had adopted more of a Leveraging Difference approach. The impetus for focusing on diversity at New Frontiers came from one of its divisions. That division's managing director constantly sought to gain competitive advantage for her division and the firm by growing her client base. Periodically, she held brain-"raging" meetings with her senior leaders in which they tackled critical strategic issues for the division. Her leadership team was meticulously crafted. She had recruited a strategically diverse set of leaders of varying age and industry experience. Because younger clients were likely to have career paths that would lead them to build wealth differently from their parents, she wanted a generationally diverse team. And she wanted team members who had work experience with industry competitors, reasoning that they could all learn from other business models. The best innovations, she reasoned, would come from a team with a common understanding of the industry but varied approaches to getting things done.

In their meetings about growing the client base, one team member pushed the notion that significant growth could come not only from reaching more households but also from building deeper loyalty within a household so that the firm would get business from one generation to the next. His previous firm had begun to gather data on generational dynamics, and it had looked promising. The New Frontiers team began experimenting with marketing that emphasized this household penetration approach. They discovered that culture and subculture predisposed some households to even greater cross-generational loyalty, and they realized that by targeting those households they might achieve even stronger client growth. As the division garnered success, company leadership was eager to transmit the same practices throughout the firm. Other divisions and managing directors embraced the approach as well, with varying degrees of success.

The New Frontiers story is a Leveraging Difference story, and clear contrasts emerge in comparison with AMEXCO. First, this difference-related change was clearly driven by a strategic objective—in this case, growing the client base. The activity New Frontiers undertook didn't come from a leader's passion to help women or people of color, nor did it mimic competitors' best practices in diversity (a common Managing Diversity activity). What New Frontiers did was focus on creating sustainable competitive advantage. If it could penetrate households across generations, it could build business in the coming decades.

New Frontiers was focused on long-term business success. In contrast to AMEXCO, it didn't worry as much about short-term pressures when approaching difference. Creating sustainable value was paramount. And accountability for this work rested solely with the management responsible for core business processes; there were no diversity officers or structures. Indeed, New Frontiers never labeled the change they were undertaking as a diversity effort. Rather, it was a business innovation activity.

Finally, New Frontiers addressed a variety of differences in counterintuitive ways. It focused on generational differences as well as cultural differences. As they delved even more deeply into the issue, team members learned a great deal about the role of gender as well; many of their high-value client prospects were older women who had outlived their husbands and now controlled the family wealth. To explore different aspects of their initiatives, New Frontiers tapped their younger employees; they sought talented women and people of color as financial advisors with the understanding that they could be instrumental in cultivating relationships with clients and in helping other stakeholders learn how to develop these clients.

### Scope of Differences Engaged

The cases of AMEXCO and New Frontiers reveal something about the kinds of differences that emerge as important in a Managing Diversity frame and a Leveraging Difference frame. AMEXCO sought and hired a director of diversity who was African American and who had strong relations with underrepresented minority groups. This is not unusual; a majority of diversity professionals in Fortune 100 companies are either people of color or white women. At New Frontiers, the relevant differences that emerged included age, culture, and gender. But other differences were equally important. Work experience with competitors was vital. Openness to unconventional thinking turned out to be pivotal.

This underscores a critical difference: Managing Diversity focuses on a limited, more traditional set of differences, while Leveraging Difference can more easily incorporate a larger set of differences.

When organizations began to pay more attention to employee diversity, it became clear that there were lots of ways in which people differ. It also quickly became clear that these differences weren't viewed as equally important or legitimate in the diversity discussion. One white male executive relayed the story of how he was "scolded" when, during a diversity discussion, he likened the challenges of being a person of color to having red hair when he was a kid. When he told of feeling different because of his hair color, he thought it would be a source of bonding with his colleagues of color. He was shocked and confused to find out that they felt belittled by his story.

This executive failed to understand where the comparison between race/ethnicity and hair color broke down. He missed the fact that whereas his hair color changed as he got older, his colleagues' cultural group memberships did not. He failed to appreciate that the social, political, and legal limitations placed on people of color were never applied based on their hair color. It became clearer to him as he talked with his colleagues that there wasn't really a "red-haired" identity in the same way there was an identity for minority groups.

Through ongoing dialogue, the executive discovered more about the many diverse dimensions of difference. Differences certainly may be based on demographics such as race, gender, or age. But they are also based on functional differences, personality, attitudes and values, cognition, and even emotional states. Each of these has been shown to affect individual and group performance in organizations.[8] With this in mind, the limitations of the Managing Diversity approach become increasingly apparent. Focusing almost exclusively on a handful of demographic differences—race, gender, national origin, religion, age, color, disability, sexual orientation, generation, class, veteran status—means ignoring many differences that matter to organizational effectiveness. It also means that people who embody and value other differences often feel discounted and excluded from their organizations' diversity efforts.

In a survey of U.S. executives and managers, the differences most of them associate with "diversity" invariably are the ones listed in the previous paragraph.[9] It is neither surprising nor inherently bad that these eleven differences demand focus (most organizations usually focus on only a subset of these differences). They are most strongly associated with historical and political struggles for equality, and with the diversity work that organizations have undertaken over the past few decades. They represent the pressing social and legal issues of the day in the United States, and few organizations can legitimately argue that they are dealing with diversity if they aren't dealing with some or all of these differences.

This smaller set of demographic differences consistently dominates the strategy and activities of Managing Diversity organizations. Even within this set, some emerge as priorities; it is difficult to establish a legitimate diversity agenda in U.S. organizations without dealing with race, ethnicity, and gender. The problem arises when the focus on these differences keeps leaders and organizations from exploring how other differences may affect performance.

In a globally competitive marketplace, the differences that should take strategic priority can shift dramatically. When a company chooses to build a new business in a different country or community, that decision must change the diversity conversation in the company. But when a Managing Diversity frame dominates, the focus often doesn't change; it remains on the relatively small set of traditional differences.

With Leveraging Difference, however, the scope can widen to include any kind of difference. Differences between marketing and sales departments, introverts and extroverts, or even legacy firms and their acquirers are all potentially relevant. Since the choice of differences to be engaged is determined by organizational strategy, many possible differences could dominate discussion and activities. Global organizations are frequently faced with the challenge of making sense of multiple differences that demand attention simultaneously. When the U.K.-based Wolseley Company acquired businesses in the United States, Canada, France, Ireland, Italy, Switzerland, the Netherlands, Eastern Europe, and four Nordic countries, the differences that preoccupied the company included both the variety of national cultures and the many corporate cultures that needed to be integrated into a unified corporate entity.

With all of these possibilities for leveraging difference, a subtle temptation might emerge. Leaders and organizations often find it easy to avoid dealing with demographic differences like race and gender because they are so difficult. A Leveraging Difference frame could be seen as a rationale for not dealing with the strategic challenges presented by inequities based on race or gender or other traditional differences. But the fact that a Leveraging Difference frame doesn't focus exclusively on these differences doesn't mean they are unimportant. A cogent Leveraging Difference strategy could very well require leaders to deal exclusively with the intractable challenges of gender or race. But the Leveraging Difference frame, unlike its counterpart, never assumes these are the only kinds of difference that matter.

## The Impact of Change

One of the assumptions underlying this book is that leaders and organizations can change for the better by exploiting differences. Therefore it is helpful to look at the differences in outcomes—in the real change—that each frame approach promotes.

### *Representation*

No matter which approach is adopted by an organization, having the desired representation of diversity is essential. Managing Diversity tactics are geared toward increasing the actual numbers of people who are different, especially with regard to demographic differences like gender, race, and age. When well executed, activity in Managing Diversity organizations does just that—recall FedTech's effort to recruit managers of color. They did change their demographic representation for a time. But the attrition that followed encapsulates the dilemma in the Managing Diversity approach: the changes are difficult to sustain.

In a Leveraging Difference frame, similar dramatic changes in demographic representation can take place—with two differences. First, the *kinds* of differences that are addressed vary; they are not just traditional demographic differences, but can also be skill-based, experiential, and even stylistic differences. Second, the strategically driven changes that take place as a result tend to last longer than the changes evident in organizations with strong Managing Diversity frames. People who are different are entering an environment that has already begun to reshape itself to be accommodating to them.

For example, eight years ago the leadership of the Progressive Graduate School of Education* decided that it was a strategic imperative to hire more faculty of color. They were focused on projections of student body makeup in the coming ten years. Given the increases in people of color in the United States (especially Hispanics) and the school's desire to have a larger global representation in its student body, they established a priority of hiring more faculty of color.

When the first faculty member of color was hired, the dean supported her with appropriate resources and mentoring by other senior faculty. Moreover, when the newly hired faculty member commented that it was untenable for her to remain as the only person of color, school leaders took her reflection seriously. Because they anticipated the turnover among tenured faculty in the coming several years, they decided to seek out faculty of color who could fill two more faculty positions immediately. Two high-quality candidates, both of color, were recruited and hired.

Investing resources in these hires revealed a long-term commitment to change by the school. This was especially true given that the positions were structured to lead to tenure, which meant permanent employment and a stake in the ongoing development of the institution. All of those faculty members remain a part of the school as of the publication of this book, and three more faculty of color have joined since, drawn to the school in part by its visible commitment. Although this institution would not be described as one that fully leverages difference, the visionary steps it took in managing talent positioned it to leverage difference more fully in the future.

### *Organizational Change*

Not surprisingly, sustainable change in an organization is more difficult to achieve under a Managing Diversity approach than it is under Leveraging Difference. In a Managing Diversity frame, change is focused on talent management. Organizations can struggle to sustain changes in representation when recruiting people who have been traditionally excluded. Even when incentives are put in place to bring in these people, there is little incentive to figure out what made the organization inhospitable to them in the first place. More critically, even if there is an emergent motivation to try to change the organization to engage people who are different, there are insufficient resources to do so.

The deeper reason that Managing Diversity organizations struggle with long-term change is that Managing Diversity approaches often are not credible drivers of change to many stakeholders. When diversity-focused changes are not clearly connected to the organization's core strategy, deep change becomes risky. Organizations exist, thrive, and grow based on a careful alignment of organizational mission, leadership, practices, systems, and culture. Prudence dictates that this alignment shouldn't be mucked with capriciously—there has to be a compelling strategic reason to change. For too many stakeholders, Managing Diversity approaches do not provide that compelling reason.

This is precisely why a Leveraging Difference frame can more successfully drive the critical incentive that is needed to sustain difference-based change. Leveraging Difference provides that connection between strategy and diversity. The way the organization looks and acts can change because its stakeholders understand and believe that the change will make the organization better. That understanding instills the commitment and energy required for enduring change and innovation. Driving such change requires creative thinking, careful planning, and a willingness to take risks. When creativity and risk aren't valued, as is often the case in a Managing Diversity world, it's no wonder that sustained change is difficult.

#### *Resistance to Change*

No matter which approach an organization adopts, there *will* be change; and with change comes resistance. As virtually all thoughtful leaders and practitioners of change attest, the more you can diminish resistance to change, the more likely it is that new ways of working will take hold.

How resistance manifests also distinguishes the two approaches. In Managing Diversity, the dynamics of defiance are well documented: resentment, passive-aggressive behavior, inertia, confusion, incivility, and claims of reverse discrimination are all indicators that resistance is alive and well.[10] Indeed, real change toward a more diverse and inclusive organization can be so threatening that even proponents of change can fall into unconscious patterns of collusion that stymie the change.

At Worldview Studios, members of the small team staffing the office of diversity were passionate and committed to creating a more diverse and inclusive company. In our interviews, they discussed tactics for making modifications and spoke articulately about the need to "carefully" bring people along, especially those who were "not on board with diversity." But when I observed them engaging with stakeholders, they were subtly confrontational, and at times they would "guilt-trip" members of the senior leadership team into acceding to some of their requests. Those leaders didn't want to push back publicly, but they would drag their feet, even though they had agreed to act. This simply fueled the diversity team's belief that the leaders needed to be pushed to action. This cycle of resistance kept the organization from achieving any substantive diversity goals.[11]

Concentrated, strong opposition to change occurs because Managing Diversity makes it quite clear who's being advocated for and who isn't. Managing Diversity explicitly or implicitly supports people in groups that are historically disaffected and disenfranchised. For example, women, people of color, gays and lesbians, disabled people—all of these individuals—would be supported by Managing Diversity efforts. But men, whites, heterosexuals, and able-bodied people are either excluded or *feel* excluded from the benefits of many Managing Diversity activities. This feeling of exclusion intensifies and reifies resistance. It becomes easier to look around, identify people like oneself, and galvanize against the change (strength in numbers).

Resistance is still present with Leveraging Difference, but it is neither as intense nor as concentrated. More stakeholders are included in both the rationale for and the implementation of the changes. Because the change is strategy-driven and aligned with the organization's purpose, the benefits that will accrue are better understood. Thus people feel more included in the change. This sense of inclusion is especially important if the change effort highlights one difference rather than another, in which case those who don't possess the relevant difference could feel slighted. But research on perceptions of justice and change reveal that people are more accepting of change if there is a credible, good-faith effort to explain the rationale behind it.[12] Leveraging Difference helps provide that rationale. The transparent and inclusive drivers of change make resistance less powerful and acceptance for the long run more likely.

### *Learning*

One outcome that is evident in both approaches is learning. In recent years, thought leaders and practitioners have emphasized the importance of learning in generating any meaningful outcomes when it comes to diversity and difference.[13] But how learning unfolds in the different frames is quite distinctive. Both produce change, but Leveraging Difference better creates the foundation for enduring change.

In Managing Diversity the strongest learning tends to take place for individuals and groups, not the organization as a whole. Diversity activities and initiatives are likely to require individuals to interact based on their differences. As varieties of identity distinctions are discussed, people begin to reflect on dimensions of difference they may not have thought about before, and insights emerge. Misconceptions and fears about engaging "different others" can be confronted. This interaction might happen while two individuals collaborate in doing the work of the organization, or it could happen simply because they both attend a particularly effective diversity training session. Whatever the impetus, this learning experience is often very powerful, sometimes even life altering.

But such learning has its limits. First, the intensity of this learning is often asymmetric: people who are in the majority tend to experience more powerful, eye-opening learning than those who are in the minority, or different. This is so because being in the majority makes it difficult to see and understand the experiences of people who aren't in the majority; majority status creates blind spots.[14] So not everyone is well positioned to experience powerful insights. Second, extending this individual learning beyond the project team or training event has proven to be more difficult under Managing Diversity. People typically emerge from their "learning laboratories" (projects or training) to find that in the larger organization it's business as usual, and the opportunities for sharing knowledge and changing how things work are limited.

Under Leveraging Difference, powerful individual learning happens, but it can happen more broadly and for more people. Since there is a broader menu of differences in play, a Hispanic woman isn't always the "minority person" whose identity and culture are the topic of the difference conversation. In the Leveraging Difference frame, her ethnicity may turn out to be less important than her limited international experience, and she may be in a position to achieve dramatic learning about doing business in Asia. Or a heterosexual senior white male mentor and a younger gay mentee may both teach and learn powerful lessons.

But a Leveraging Difference frame provides another powerful learning opportunity because it positions an organization to take advantage of differences that may emerge in the future as the world changes, accompanied by social and business changes. For example, in the United States national culture differences were much less relevant forty years ago when the economic focus was more heavily on the domestic market. With increasing global competition and opportunity, cultural differences now matter a great deal more. Companies that learned how to capitalize on differences that were relevant in 1970 (for example, gender and race) can now apply some of those lessons as they are confronted with cross-national differences. Put another way, operating under a Leveraging Difference frame helps organizations develop a capability for engaging and using difference to achieve its goals. That capability becomes woven into the fabric of the organization. It can become standard operating procedure.

### The Intersection of Managing Diversity and Leveraging Difference

Outlining the distinctions between Managing Diversity and Leveraging Difference creates a natural dualism. It becomes easy to see two distinct approaches and to compare them in an effort to choose the superior one. In fact, I have fostered this dualism in these early chapters as I've attempted to build the argument that a Leveraging Difference approach will generate superior outcomes to a Managing Diversity approach. But while I hold fast to the notion that some elements of Managing Diversity actually hinder efforts to truly realize the power of diversity, Managing Diversity has been useful historically for a reason. It has helped generate a blueprint for one way to work with difference. Some elements of that blueprint will be useful in creating a new Leveraging Difference blueprint.

Throughout the remainder of this book, I will advocate building on Managing Diversity techniques rather than completely discarding them. As we examine the steps leading to Leveraging Difference, it will be apparent that while the two models are distinct, they are not always mutually exclusive. This is one of the many cases in which it would be unwise to throw the baby out with the bathwater.

## What Next?

Efforts to create more dynamic, inclusive, and effective organizations are thwarted because too many characteristics of the Managing Diversity approach plague twenty-first-century organizations. Managing Diversity has served as the foundation for creating more diverse and inclusive organizations over the past four decades, but it has become a substantial impediment to the kind of change needed to propel organizations in an increasingly global and complex business environment. Leveraging Difference provides a powerful, globally applicable way to address and sustain diversity and inclusion in the twenty-first century.

The critical question is: how?

## Key Takeaways

1. Leveraging Difference is defined as taking action within an organization to use people's differences to help the organization achieve its strategic goals.
2. Leveraging Difference provides a different way of thinking about diversity, one that is necessary in today's increasingly global and complex business environment.
3. Organizational approaches to diversity can be divided into two approaches: the traditional "Managing Diversity" method and what I propose as a "Leveraging Difference" approach. These are the central differences between the two:

*Context*—Managing Diversity is U.S.-focused, while Leveraging Difference more easily applies to global contexts.

*Leadership Orientation*—Managing Diversity is problem-focused, whereas Leveraging Difference is opportunity-focused.

*Strategic Focus*—In Managing Diversity, diversity almost always is an HR/talent issue. In Leveraging Difference, "difference activity" is driven by business strategy and can focus on talent, operations, marketing, and external alliances or partnerships.

*Scope of Differences*—While Managing Diversity focuses on a limited, traditional set of differences, Leveraging Difference can more easily incorporate a larger set of differences.

*Degree of Sustainable Change*—Changes tend to last longer under the Leveraging Difference approach because the environment has already begun to reshape itself to accommodate the differences that are now in play. Transparent and inclusive drivers of change make resistance less powerful and acceptance for the long run more likely. Leveraging Difference helps organizations develop a capability for using differences to achieve their goals, something that becomes woven into the fabric of the organization.

4. Managing Diversity is not an incorrect approach. Rather, it is less relevant in a global marketplace. That is why Leveraging Difference can be more powerful in dealing with difference.

# 3

# The Leveraging Difference Capability

*By Martin N. Davidson & Heather R. Wishik*

Even as I was excited to take on my new position as chief diversity officer at Darden, one unattractive project had fallen into my lap. The university administration had created an ambitious action plan to raise the diversity profile at the institution. This included a large-scale program to be held at the business school examining the impact of race and ethnicity on economics and business. It was a great idea, but one that required substantial resources. Part of my job was to generate those resources.

To that end, I welcomed to Darden Mark Settles, then managing director and director of executive recruiting at JPMorgan Chase. Darden and JPMorgan Chase were interested in deepening their institutional relationship, and exploring the diversity domain was one way to do that. Settles was a fascinating guest—extremely curious, with a sharp intellect and a warm personal style. He seemed to enjoy his visit and dived right in with questions to key stakeholders, trying to figure out the best link between Darden and his firm. My goal was to help him see why Chase should invest in our program.

The day was great, and at the end of the visit we sat together to talk about what we could do. I was eager to hear what he had to say, and I ready to disabuse him of any notion that we were not a top-notch institution committed to diversity. But I never got the chance—he immediately confirmed that we were a top-notch institution. So I asked him what more we needed to do to persuade JPMorgan Chase to invest in us. He said, "We're looking to invest in schools that are not only committed to diversity, but are living it."

I asked him to elaborate. He said he wanted us to be the kind of place where, whether he was talking to the dean or to an academic secretary or to facilities staff, people knew what diversity meant at Darden—what our commitment was, and what we were doing to further that commitment. "Here's my example," he said. "When I ask someone about the Consortium [a preeminent organization for promoting diversity and inclusion in American business and business education], everyone in the institution should know what it is and what Darden's relationship to it is."

He went on. "My point is that we want to partner with institutions where diversity is a given, not an add-on. You guys are good. I want you to be better."

## The Leveraging Difference Capability

Settles was offering something more valuable than funding for a program. He was challenging us to move beyond a temporary program, or a change initiative to be embarked upon, completed, and then forgotten. One of the great dilemmas of a Managing Diversity approach is that the activity it generates in an organization is frequently uncoordinated, highly tactical, and rarely sustained. To combat this, an organization has to develop a way of relating to difference that becomes deeply embedded into the fabric of the organization. It is not enough to simply tolerate or even welcome difference. Rather, it must *live* difference. This requires cultivating an enduring way for an organization and its people to operate in relation to difference. Drawing from the language of organizational strategists, today's organizations must develop an *organizational capability* for difference.

An organizational capability is a collection of knowledge and-skills that are embedded in, and supported by, the organization's people, practices, and systems. A few examples of organizational capabilities are being able to make important changes rapidly, collaborate across organizational boundaries and silos, and manage costs efficiently. A capability becomes valuable when it is directly useful in helping the organization achieve its fundamental mission, strategy, and goals. For profit-making companies, that means the capability helps the company maintain an advantage over industry competitors. For a nonprofit, it may mean that it helps the organization remain sustainable so it can continuously execute on its mission. Organizational capabilities equip the organization to do what it needs to do in order to achieve results.

Developing a capability for difference is critical for organizations in the twenty-first century. The purpose of an organization—whether profit-making, governmental, or not-for-profit—is to achieve some goal, to deliver some product or service desired by the people and entities with which the organization interacts. Organizations create value for their stakeholders. The problem is that the set of stakeholders in the modern world is more explicitly diverse than ever before. Technology has made it increasingly evident that people of many cultures, perspectives, and interests are now customers, employees, advocates, and leaders. It is no longer a

**Figure 1 The Leveraging Difference Cycle**

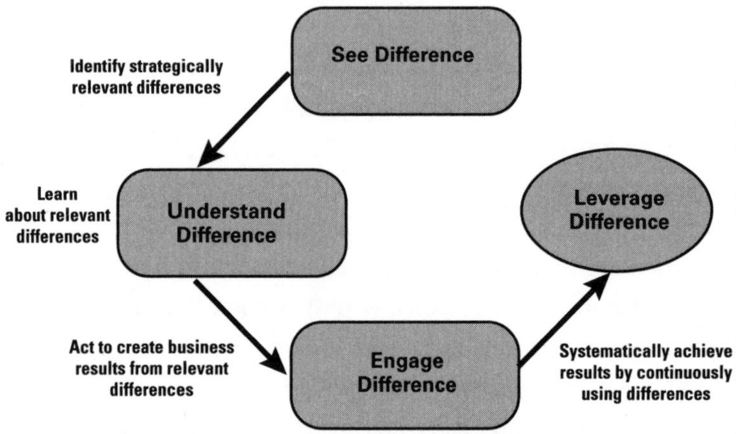


viable strategy to marginalize or ignore the diversity they embody. As a result, there is a heightened need for collaboration among all these diverse individuals, groups, organizations, and societies in order to address the pressing problems and opportunities present in the world.[1] Navigating this diversity in productive, ethical, and empowering ways is paramount for any organization that wants to be truly world-class.

Therefore organizations must develop reliable and powerful ways of relating to difference that embed it into the core operation, activities, and mindset of the organization and its members. Moving through the Leveraging Difference Cycle does just that. The three components of the Leveraging Difference capability are illustrated in Figure 1: seeing, understanding, and engaging difference. Leaders and organizations that are able to develop each of these components effectively are moving closer to truly leveraging difference.

### *Seeing Difference*

Seeing difference is the means by which strategically relevant differences surface in an organization. These are the differences that presently or potentially contribute to carrying out the organization's core strategy and mission. They might be anything from cultural background to physical ability to organizational differences between collaborating firms. Whether or not these differences are relevant depends on the organization's strategy, so seeing difference begins with having a clear understanding of that strategy. Beyond that, to properly identify relevant differences, leaders must manage the forces that can distract them from focusing on the right differences.

Identifying relevant differences can be challenging because biases and blinders get in the way. For example, one critical difference can be ignored because of an emphasis on another difference. At the LLC Insurance firm,* an impending lawsuit prompted the organization to focus heavily on race in the hope that it could stave off litigation. They poured a great deal of time, energy, and effort into doing this. But an unintended outcome of that effort was that white women in the organization became increasingly frustrated because the organization was neglecting their problems, such as limited advancement opportunities.

At other times, one difference is emphasized over another because the Managing Diversity mindset, with its focus on traditional differences, crowds out serious consideration of any other difference, even if they are really important to performance. At Takata Corporation, a manufacturer of safety systems for automobiles, the challenges of Irish immigrants working in a southeast U.S. plant were underemphasized because it was assumed they would figure out how to fit in. The plant's leaders weren't seeing a relevant difference—national cultural background—that was important to the plant's functioning.

Similarly, ensuring that the relevant difference is identified can be challenging if energy is diverted elsewhere—if leaders have focused their attention on a difference that is actually less relevant. Or resources may be invested in diversity-related activities that, while potentially valuable, don't contribute directly to obtaining the needed difference. In essence, seeing difference is the Leveraging Difference component that gives the organization something to work with.

### *Understanding Difference*

Identifying relevant differences and getting the right people into the organization does not guarantee that key stakeholders will know how to make sense of the differences. Understanding requires learning about the nature of the difference and how it could affect any aspect of the organization: employees, customers, products and services, operational effectiveness, and communities. The key to understanding difference is developing personal and organizational competencies for learning about difference. Those competencies are best developed through collaboration and relationships between people who are different, even if they don't necessarily represent the particular difference under consideration. The failure to foster a strong general sense of collaboration between people and between groups frequently derails specific diversity efforts and larger organizational performance. When people can't overcome barriers to collaboration across their own differences, they can't be open to learning about other differences that matter. Without understanding difference, people of diverse backgrounds and perspectives quickly become estranged from one another.

The leadership team of a Russian division of Barrimore Corporation,* a global manufacturer of household products, was made up entirely of Indian and Dutch managers. But the bulk of the workforce was predominantly Russian. The leaders struggled with their employees' easygoing style and apparent unwillingness to take initiative, worrying that this was a symptom of widespread disengagement that was affecting performance. But Russian employees, many of whom were quite accomplished, noted that what the leaders labeled as disengagement was actually reticence to challenge authority, something the workers had learned under years of authoritarian social and governmental control. The division leaders' failure to understand the impact of this historical reality kept them from creatively dealing with the perceived lack of initiative among the Russians.

In another instance, MFB Retailers* hired a cadre of African American sales and marketing managers because they served a large black customer base. After several quarters of consistently subpar sales performance, they realized that they had made a mistake. While the region had been exclusively African American through the 1990s, the black customer base in 2007 included significant immigrant and second-generation communities from Haiti, Jamaica, and Ghana. And the African Americans the company had hired were not knowledgeable about the circumstances and tastes of these other black communities. The leaders of this firm didn't understand the diversity within the market they wanted to exploit.

These are examples of leaders and organizations struggling to move beyond the labels for differences—"Russian," "black," and so on—provided in the seeing stage of the Leveraging Difference Cycle. These labels are shorthand; they can help an organization measure its progress in increasing the representation of various categories. The problem comes when organizations don't skillfully gather data about the labeled difference in order to understand how and why it matters to the business. Failing to understand the nature of a seen difference, or making faulty assumptions about the nature of the difference, stalls any progress toward leveraging that difference.

The extent to which understanding difference occurs also depends on having organizational systems that support it. People learn about difference as individuals and in relationships, but organizations can also institutionalize the acquisition of that knowledge. For example, many organizations support informal employee groups that organize around group identity, technical skill, or functional expertise. These can be sources of understanding when the core difference is identified as one that is strategically relevant at a given business moment.

### *Engaging Difference*

Seeing difference and understanding difference are important steps in the Leveraging Difference process because they establish a sense of urgency. The link between seeing difference and achieving strategic goals is part of the reason for that urgency. Leaders begin to make connections between the relevant difference and achieving strategic results, even if they cannot capitalize on those connections yet.

As this process unfolds, people become increasingly motivated to change because they feel greater connection to and have greater insight into the differences embodied by their colleagues and friends. The social transformations that often occur in the understanding difference step heighten that urgency. As people navigate relationships through their differences and establish deeper connections, they are more motivated to change how they operate. They just aren't sure what to do yet.

The transformative experiences stemming from seeing and understanding difference catapult leaders into engaging difference—trying to use relevant differences to create tangible results. At this step, leaders begin to act in coordinated ways. They put into place experiments that might leverage important differences. At Worldview Studios, leaders decided that ongoing tensions between older and younger employees—Baby Boomers and Generation Y'ers—was becoming more of a problem than a humorous distraction. Team collaboration was breaking down and conflict was increasing. Leaders decided to intervene by creating "cross-mentoring" relationships between selected senior and junior employees. The pairs met for facilitated training twice a year to help establish skills for communication, listening, counseling, and conflict management. Each pair had an assigned coach to whom they had access at any time. Post-program assessments showed improved understanding of generational issues by both parties, and strengthened relationships among all the pairs. As information about the program spread, interest was piqued throughout the organization. Participants shared insights in team meetings and in a regular employee interest column/blog on the company intranet. The company began planning a second program.

Engaging difference is the place of experimentation in which change begins. It requires 1) committing to the importance of the business opportunities offered by a given difference or set of differences, and 2) acting on that commitment to capitalize on the difference by experimenting with new ways of doing things. Engaging difference is a powerful learning experience. It has a "trial and error" quality to it as leaders and organizations attempt to figure out what it means to incorporate critical differences that could affect results. And it encourages leaders to examine assumptions about difference in the organization that otherwise might never surface. Ultimately, it prepares leaders for doing what they believe has a chance to be strategically effective. This is a challenging crossroads, because if the opportunity presented by a difference seems important enough, they must choose to change even when the need to do so may not be apparent to everyone.

Many leaders make the mistake of assuming that engaging difference is the desired endpoint for effectively leveraging difference. But when leaders and companies are merely engaging difference, they are still involved in tactical activity. They are feeling their way, trying out programs, policies, or training curricula that may or may not create incremental change. The difference between engaging and leveraging is that leveraging difference is the manifestation of a new capability, one that integrates difference-related activities into the organization's core capabilities.

### *Leveraging Difference*

The full-circle conclusion of the cycle happens when leaders and their organizations experience a quantum shift. The organization is no longer just experimenting but is, in fact, "living difference." When leaders and organizations are leveraging difference in a sustained way, the use of difference to generate results becomes increasingly effortless. The organization begins to orient itself toward determining how differences can contribute to results, doing so as a regular practice. Learning about the implications of difference becomes a pervasive approach to doing business.

Ultimately, creating sustained results by leveraging difference requires leaders to make sure that every part of the organization sees, understands, and engages difference. The cycle must be integrated into the way planning, strategy development, and decision-making are conducted. This can be a great opportunity for the organization. Positive results breed energy and commitment. Stakeholders begin to talk openly about what they are doing, using the language of Leveraging Difference. Moreover, part of adopting the Leveraging Difference capability is committing to the continued use of the cycle to explore new relevant differences.

A capability comes to life when it serves to generate high performance by being used. Simply having a capability doesn't make it especially valuable. In fact, having a capability that doesn't further the execution of a company's strategy can lead to a wasteful activity. Frequently this is exactly what happens with diversity in organizations.

### The Case of Wipro Technologies

Companies that use a Leveraging Difference capability to its fullest remain rare. However, the power of that capability is visible in a variety of companies that rely on difference as a competitive advantage. Wipro Technologies is one of those companies.[2]

Wipro is an India-based global IT services business arm of Wipro Ltd. In 1980 Wipro Ltd. started offering information technology services in India. Just three years later—the same year that Microsoft started up—Wipro entered the software market. By the late 1980s, the company found its growth business—software services—and had earned contracts as a software integrator with General Electric, Cisco Systems, Sun Microsystems, Hitachi, and Alcatel. Wipro and General Electric formed Wipro GE Medical Systems as a joint venture. The firm continued to develop joint ventures with other partners, and in 1995 Wipro joined forces with Taiwan-based Acer to manufacture and sell computers and peripherals in India.

By 1999 Wipro had reorganized into four separately run groups: software (called Wipro Technologies); hardware and systems; consumer care and lighting; and hydraulic fluid. It also formed Wipro Net to offer e-commerce implementation services. Despite these changes, company headquarters remained in Bangalore, India. In July 1999, Vivek Paul became president of Wipro Technologies. Wipro Ltd. CEO Azim Premji's goal for Wipro Technologies was for it to be one of the top ten IT service providers in the world by 2010, and he wanted Paul to lead the way.

Paul decided immediately that he would locate his own office in California, in Silicon Valley. He commented, "If we want to be a player in IT services, we need a U.S. presence. Having Wipro Technologies' headquarters in California means more travel for me, since I have to go back to India frequently, but it is better for the company."

Premji and Paul were determined to reduce Wipro Technologies' heavy dependence on the U.S. economy as quickly as possible. To grow the business globally, Paul knew he needed someone at the helm who had established relationships and held credibility with people in Wipro Technologies' Indian operations centers—someone who knew the Indian operational culture and had the cross-cultural sophistication that came from extended expatriate experience. Sudip Nandy—a respected and accomplished Wipro manager—was the perfect fit for such an assignment, and Paul was very pleased when he accepted the offer to be European director of sales and marketing in early 2000.

When Nandy arrived in Europe, Wipro's small European operation, headquartered in London, was ready to grow. It looked like a global company because it had customers in several countries. But Nandy's portfolio was essentially Western Europe, covering primarily Scandinavia, the United Kingdom, Ireland, Germany, France, Austria, and Switzerland, with smaller business operations in Italy and Spain, and the Benelux countries. He hoped to increase Wipro's presence farther east to include Poland, Hungary, Estonia, and Latvia.

Although the firm's customers were global in early 2000, Wipro's European sales, marketing, and project management staff were all Indian expatriates. Many employees had been in Europe a relatively short time. Sales were made to European clients; contracts were developed at the client's site; and then the work orders were sent back to India to be completed. This was the competitive value proposition Wipro Technologies could offer: the highest-quality technological depth and customized services, delivered by cheaper Indian labor.

The Indian employees in Europe maintained their collegial relationships with each other and with their counterparts in India, who implemented the contracts and projects. As a result, employees did not quickly build networks in the local communities. As excellent as the Indian team in Europe was, Nandy knew that growing the European business was going to require more knowledge of the subtleties of the local markets than this staff could possibly develop on its own. Besides, many of Wipro's competitors already had strong customer relationships in many of the European countries. According to Paul, major competitors "had a good business understanding in terms of the local business situations and the business context of technology."

Premji had made it clear to everyone at Wipro Technologies that being truly global meant not only operating in multiple countries, but doing so with the "face of the country." When Paul hired Nandy, he warned that the biggest challenge would be hiring and nurturing the right people for each country. One of Nandy's earliest priorities was to hire locals with knowledge of various business sectors in specific countries. The idea was to integrate Indian and local cultures into Wipro's Euro sales, marketing, and account and customer relations management. Nandy had to do this without making the Indian members of the team feel less valued. One approach he used was having them participate in the hiring of the locals and in suggesting where locals would be most useful. Nandy explained:

> That was a really tricky thing—when you are hiring a lot of locals and your current business is completely dependent on nonlocals whom you have moved from India—ensuring that they don't feel threatened. I think I hit it off with the existing team right away because they knew I was an old Wipro hand and I wouldn't screw them. So the portfolio essentially is to be able to make Wipro Europe become a nonentity. I want it to be Wipro Germany, Wipro UK, and Wipro France. My mission is to get my team at least 60/40: 60 percent Indians who had previously come to Europe and 40 percent new local people they hire.

Nandy knew that integrating Europeans and Indians was going to be challenging. The cultural fit was complex and not easy to achieve. The task was not simply for Indian and European colleagues working together face-to-face in Europe to learn how to work with each other. The Europeans, hired for their European client relationships and business acumen, had to quickly learn how to build working relationships with project managers, engineers, and teams of Indians working in India. Europeans had to help shepherd the relationships between Wipro's clients and the India-based Wipro people. The India-based staff would periodically come to Europe, but more often they used e-mail, the telephone, and videoconferencing. And India-based employees were critical participants on the Wipro side of contract negotiations with clients, as well as providers of the actual IT services to the clients once a contract was in place.

Highly functional relationships between the Indian- and Europe-based staffs set up conditions for successful negotiation of client contracts. The European account managers needed India-based knowledge to appropriately manage client expectations and guarantee customer satisfaction. The Europeans, no matter what their role, also had to understand Indian business culture in general and Wipro's Indian operational culture in particular. Finally, the clients themselves needed to learn more about Indian culture and business operations if their interactions with Indian personnel at Wipro were going to be successful.

Nandy realized he needed some new models. Many of Wipro Technologies' early clients were large global firms with a long history of working with Indian software engineers. Even with relatively sophisticated clients, Nandy watched Wipro Technologies and other Indian companies in the United States struggle to find the right Americans for their sales forces. So in Europe he decided to look for locals "who have sufficient grasp of the abstract, tolerance for ambiguity, and the patience to be able to grow with us for one year." He searched for critical core personal characteristics, including some typical of people from India—"for instance, your resilience, your ability to remain calm, your ability to deal with uncertainty, such as juggling changes in schedules."

"I think those are good things," Nandy said. "I remember an article that was written abroad saying that Indians do very well elsewhere because they deal better with uncertainty, because people from India are used to uncertainty." Nandy also worked with his Indian team to be open to building relationships with their new European counterparts. "I know that locals will force us to think differently, do things differently, get more blatant at times, get more subtle at other times."

Creating a proper induction program for his new European hires was critical. Nandy decided to send each new employee to India at the outset of their employment and on a regular basis—every three to four months—"to recharge, not the batteries, but the contacts." Nandy continued:

> And again to understand what we are. You don't get a feeling for what we are unless you go there. We are like a factory, which is our main strength, and the factory is in India. So many things have got to be put in place for local hires to make them really become as much Wiprocentric as possible, because I think they are excellent salesmen in their own country. They understand what the customer's need is far better. I think the only thing to do is to understand exactly what our value proposition is and how to tweak it for the local customer.

### *Building Cultural Competence for Indian Staff*

In India, Wipro Technologies tried to build cultural understanding among the India-based staffers who worked on projects with European clients. Before any employee traveled anywhere their first time, Wipro Technologies made corporate training a prerequisite. The program consisted of one- to two-day, country-specific cross-cultural awareness courses that described business cultures by nationality. Wipro also built content based on feedback from those employees who had gone abroad without training. Returning expatriates shared their experiences, and they generally agreed that they could have been much more effective had they gone through a cross-cultural training program before they left India. As Wipro's senior executive trainer and course designer Bharathi Srinivasan explained:

> We switched over to training before traveling because we learned that people should have this sensitivity. Our people are interacting with clients over the phone, over the mail, and other communications, so we thought it was important for any individual who joins the company. Unless our people attend the training sessions they cannot travel—they don't get their tickets if they don't enter this program, to that level it has become mandatory.

Indian employees were enrolled in language programs. The idea was to understand what a German or French client was saying and to be able to speak a few sentences and ask a few questions. Differences between British and American English were also highlighted.

### *Teaching the Client How to Partner with Wipro and Work with Indians*

Another plan that Nandy hoped would create success in Europe involved clients. Nandy asked his salespeople to encourage clients who lacked experience with South Asian partners to learn more about Indian culture. One strategy was to request as a term of the contract that the client pay for their own learning through use of a consultant designated by Wipro, an American cultural trainer familiar with Indian business culture. So when Wipro won the contract to provide information systems design and management for the Scottish Parliament, the consultant's services were written into the contract. She worked with the internal partners at the Parliament who handled most of the interactions with Wipro Technologies' India-based people. The idea that customers needed to learn about Wipro and Indian business culture was not Nandy's invention, although his way of addressing the issue was new. Ranjan Acharya, Wipro Technologies's Bangalore-based vice president of corporate and human resource development, described how the company first expanded its learning circle to include the customer:

> I remember there was one company in the United States that invited our people to come and talk to their people every Friday on what India was all about. In their own way they were trying to learn how to deal with us and understand us as much as we were trying to understand and interact with them. We decided we had to give a wider exposure to people—get our people to stay there, get customers to come here, send some people from there to here and here to there.

Nandy realized that his non-Indian employees were astonished when they experienced India, and so were the customers. "They stay for one day and we give them at least ten presentations," he said. "Each one lasts an hour, with a short lunch, and a coffee, with no time to take a stroll or anything." So the company learned from the interactions between customers and India, and between employees and India. "It's a two-way process—therefore we are learning from that."

Nandy felt good about what his team of Indian employees had accomplished in the first year of his leadership. His group had gone from 100 percent Indian to 20 percent local European employees and 80 percent Indian. This put Nandy halfway to his goal on personnel balance. And business had grown 120 percent to 130 percent.

### *The Leveraging Difference Cycle at Wipro*

The Wipro Technologies case illustrates the power of applying a Leveraging Difference capability to business. Premji and Paul had a clear strategic goal: Wipro had to grow as an IT service provider, and it had to do so with a much greater global profile. With this aspiration in mind, they began to explore how they would use difference to help the company grow. Nandy's appointment as European director of sales and marketing signaled that the work would begin there.

The European operation was small and offered lots of growth opportunities. One difference Nandy was able to see immediately was that Wipro Europe was really Wipro Western Europe; the company had not yet moved east. Also, all of Wipro's European clients were serviced by Indian staff. This was not necessarily a bad thing; part of the Wipro value proposition was to provide cheaper high-quality service, and Indian labor was cheaper than European labor. But the savings came at the loss of customer intimacy. The Indian staff didn't really understand their clients' cultural and business contexts well enough. They were providing customer service, but they didn't really *know* their customers. And Wipro's European competitors did.

Nandy *saw* the strategically relevant differences: Indians and Europeans working together in Europe and India, and staff working collaboratively across functions and levels. Now he was focusing on *understanding* what that difference meant for the firm. He agreed with Premji that being successful globally meant having the "face of the customer," so he knew he wanted to get Europeans into the operation. What was unclear was how he would bring them in and how he would promote the collaboration he needed.

So Nandy needed to conduct what would become a series of *engaging difference* experiments. First, he hired European locals. Using his knowledge about what had worked (and what had not worked) in the United States, he used novel criteria for hiring in Europe, looking for global leadership competencies in the people he hired. To foster the collaboration he wanted, he began to experiment with sending Europeans to India and with encouraging Indians to engage in more focused learning about Europe. One result was that "Europe" became much more granular: the staff began to think in terms of Germans, French, and Dutch instead of simply Europeans. And because the internal cross-cultural learning was so powerful, they started experimenting with cross-cultural learning between customers and employees. The outcome was twofold: more effective internal collaboration and more positive and powerful client relations.

## Key Takeaways

1. Today's organizations must develop an *organizational capability* for difference: a collection of knowledge or skills embedded in, and supported by, the organization's people, practices, and systems.
2. To develop any capability, leaders and organizations must focus on three primary components: people, practices, and systems.

3. The set of stakeholders in the modern world is more diverse than ever before, requiring a heightened need for collaboration.
4. Moving through the Leveraging Difference Cycle enables organizations to develop reliable and powerful ways of relating to difference that become part of the core operation, activity, and mindset of the organization and its members.
5. The Leveraging Difference capability has three components:
   - *Seeing difference* is the means by which relevant differences are identified in the organization.
   - *Understanding difference* stems from learning about the nature of a relevant difference and how people who carry that difference experience the organization.
   - *Engaging difference* is the activity of exploring ways that a difference can be used to enhance the organization.
6. Leveraging Difference is the manifestation of a new capability that integrates difference-related activities with the core capabilities of the organization.
7. The full-circle conclusion of the cycle occurs when leaders and their organizations experience a quantum shift: the organization is no longer just experimenting but is, in fact, "living difference."

# 4

# Seeing Difference

Seeing difference is the act of identifying the differences that are strategically important for an organization. The kinds of differences that can be important to an organization vary widely. Strategic benefits might come from racial or gender diversity, but they could also come from differences in regional cultures, levels of expertise, or linguistic nuances. And a difference may be important in one context, such as operation efficiency, but not in another, like customer relations. To leverage difference well, a leader's task is to guide the organization toward focusing on and exploiting the differences that matter most, when they matter most.

Easier said than done.

Because of the emphasis on traditional differences that a Managing Diversity approach can impose, organizations and leaders working with diversity may subtly limit the differences they see as strategically important. This isn't always intentional, but it is common. With its powerful emphasis on traditional differences like race and gender, Managing Diversity can obscure more strategically important differences like country of origin, age,

**Figure 2 Seeing Difference**

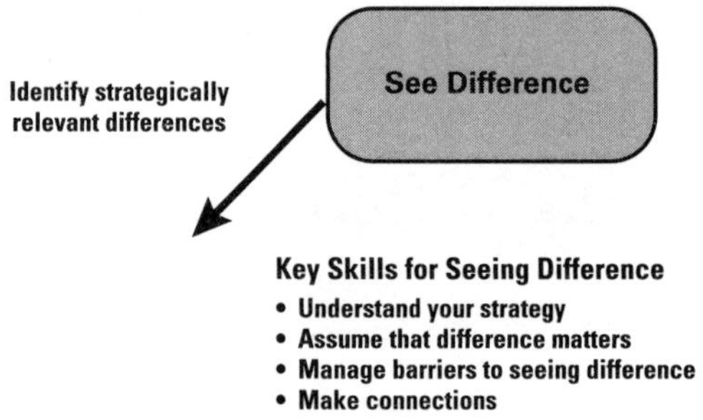


or interfirm business procedures. In this way, Managing Diversity can actually *prevent* organizations from leveraging difference.

To counteract this limitation, leaders attempting to build a Leveraging Difference capability must make sure they are identifying differences that serve their organization's strategic needs. Then they must make sure that those differences are effectively incorporated into the organization by acquiring talent and gaining knowledge.

In this chapter, I expand on some of the challenges of these tasks, as well as ways to overcome those challenges.

## The Cost of Not Seeing Relevant Differences

Organizations frequently "leave money on the table" as a result of not seeing differences clearly. In the marketplace, customers who hold different tastes pass over the standard offerings that don't satisfy those tastes. Often sellers are never even aware of the opportunities they are missing. A friend shared with me her excitement over finding "Black Angels"—holiday ornaments with dark brown skin color—at her local T. J. Maxx store. An African

American mother of two, she had been searching for Christmas ornaments that reflected her racial and cultural identity. When she found the angels, she literally bought out the store, purchasing them for herself and as gifts. Moreover, she told me and anyone else who would listen how great the T. J. Maxx chain was. How many companies in how many industries are failing to capitalize on frustrated customers with "different" tastes?

Not seeing important differences can be costly in interfirm relationships as well. Companies attempting to merge following acquisitions fail in their efforts anywhere from 65 percent to 85 percent of the time.[1] When Chrysler and Daimler-Benz became DaimlerChrysler in 1998, what evolved provides an example of the problems that can arise when stakeholders don't see the relevant differences. The post-integration team invested a good deal of resources trying to help employees understand the differences between American and German culture. They even sponsored workshops on "Sexual Harassment in the American Workplace" and "German Dining Etiquette," assuming that national culture would be the obvious relevant difference. In fact, the firm's real problems stemmed from differences in management perceptions and business practices. The two firms held different organizational values, had different compensation structures, and followed different philosophies about how to brand their products.[2] As critical as national culture was to this partnership, differences in business practices and routines, firm values, and management and employee attitudes were even more important. It is not uncommon that failing to see relevant differences impedes the integration of organizations attempting to collaborate with one another.

The cost of not seeing difference also hits home when talent is lost through turnover or disengagement. Adriana Maria Garcia

Diaz's experience illustrates this cost. Of mestizo heritage, she was born outside Quito, Ecuador, and lived there for the first three years of her life before her parents moved to Atlanta. Her father was a supply chain expert who'd been recruited by Coca-Cola Company in Georgia. Her mother had been a successful entertainer in Ecuador. Though home was now Atlanta, in her youth Diaz spent many summers back in Ecuador. She was affable and very connected to her family and her community in Ecuador as well as in Atlanta. She liked being an organizer and collaborating with people and enjoyed organizing social events. She spoke three languages: Spanish and English fluently, and the Incan language Quechua conversationally. She was beloved by her family; her mother was fond of noting that she had both a very sharp logical mind and *un espíritu sensible*—a sensitive spirit.

Diaz majored in economics and music at Emory University. She was an accomplished jazz pianist and particularly loved improvisation; she enjoyed thinking on her feet. She worked as an analyst with Bank of America before earning her MBA and starting a career in investment banking at Goldman Sachs. Despite the fact that the firm was first-rate and that she really liked her manager, she was unsettled. She was smart and well trained and had always worked hard because she was committed to excellence. Yet she wasn't advancing as quickly as some of her peers, even though she seemed to perform better than several of them.

Diaz had worked hard to build strong industry knowledge and relationships and felt that she was doing all the right things. But feedback from her managing director made it evident that she wasn't being seriously considered for promotion. She wasn't seen as someone with effective people-management skills, an assessment reinforced by her difficulty connecting with colleagues. Diaz had always been a little introverted, and at the firm she never quite felt like she was making strong connections. No one was impolite, just indifferent. This all fed into a feeling of being out of the mainstream. She was self-conscious that she wasn't a U.S. native, that she still had her Spanish accent, and that she was a female in the predominantly male world of banking. Her ongoing sense of powerlessness and feeling undervalued led her to leave the firm after six years.

This story is endemic to many organizations. Diaz's professional and cultural background was rich and complex, and she brought skills and experiences that could enhance an organization. She had been acknowledged as an extremely competent analyst with outstanding technical proficiency. But she also possessed a well-developed aptitude for managing people, politics, and egos—in her extended community and family. Outside of the bank, Diaz was seen as the ultimate manager, who motivated people with skill, managed projects well, and dealt with conflict effectively. Moreover, her musical inclinations indicated she was likely to be skilled in dealing with ambiguity. She had persevered, investing many resources—both material and psychological—in realizing a vision for her career and life. But her array of talents wasn't evident to her superiors. The firm was definitely looking for an associate with her managerial potential. But Diaz was not *seen* as management material.

This sort of obliviousness has consequences both for people like Diaz and for the firms who employ them. Hiring and developing someone who doesn't then succeed is costly. As a low performer, the employee requires a greater outlay of time and support from managers and peers. If he or she leaves, the turnover costs are high, as replacements must be recruited and trained. But perhaps the most critical costs of not being able to see all of a person's talent come in missing how she might have performed if she hadn't felt so constrained. What could someone like Diaz contribute to the firm if she were able to perform to her fullest ability? What existing networks might she leverage to bring in new business? What new networks might she enter or create? What innovative ideas might she produce? What leadership could she exert?

When someone experiences a gap between what her job requires and what she believes she could contribute, she is going to become increasingly dissatisfied. That means she is less likely to be mentally focused and energized, which can mean lower job performance. The further people begin to fall behind in performance, the more others—bosses, peers, even subordinates—begin to label her as a weak link. That label almost always gets interpreted as a product of a lack of talent rather than the possibility that she is working under a handicap. Once those labels attach, not only is it hard for others to see her as anything but a weak performer, but she starts to believe it of herself. And the more she believes she cannot perform, the more she really cannot perform. She feels increasingly anxious about whether she will be able to advance or even keep her job; she is simply unhappy. This vicious circle can push people like Adriana out of organizations even as their talent and potential contributions go unrealized.

An often overlooked fact is that this problem of not seeing an individual's difference extends not just to the Adrianas, people who differ from the majority. It may also affect "Bobs" and "Freds," people who look like mainstream white guys. Bob and Fred may also bring a host of experiences and skills that could add value to the organization. And they may also feel they are prevented from using those experiences and skills at work. It is usually tougher for the Adrianas, because they are so visibly different and thus more vulnerable to being perceived as an underperformer. But people who are different are rarely the only ones who suffer when differences are not seen.

## How to See Difference

Seeing the differences that were invisible to T. J. Maxx's competitors, to DaimlerChrysler's leaders, and to Adriana Diaz's managers and peers requires that leaders and stakeholders hone their "lenses" more finely so they can identify the differences that matter. That requires attention to four areas: clarity of strategic goals, openness to looking for difference, ability to manage biases and distortions in seeing, and ability to leverage relationships across differences.

### *Understand Your Strategy*

The foundational competency for seeing difference is identifying what difference is relevant. A relevant difference is one that is strategically meaningful to the organization and that has the potential to help it perform more effectively. For example, people with divergent thinking ability—the capacity to generate creative ideas by exploring many possible solutions—are essential for developing creative advertising campaigns. You would want to tap into this kind of difference if you were an ad agency. But knowing how to determine relevance is not a simple task.

In a Managing Diversity frame, relevant differences are usually those that belong to the list of traditional differences. Choosing a subset of those to focus on can be challenging, but the task is easier that selecting from the larger set of differences than could be in play in a Leveraging Difference frame. In order to make sense of the universe of differences that could be important to an organization, leaders need a guide to help them focus on what really matters. They need organizational strategy. Yet it is all too common for key leaders and stakeholders to be confused about what their organization's strategy really is. This goes beyond issues of difference and diversity. It is a common observation among practitioners and scholars that the people who need to be able to execute a strategy often do not have a clear understanding of what the strategy is.[3] They are undertaking activity that is productive on the face of it, but they are not connected to an overarching roadmap for the organization. Seeing difference with the goal of leveraging it requires a connection to that larger roadmap.

Making that larger roadmap accessible requires strategic tools. A comprehensive list of all the tools that can be used to develop and communicate strategy is beyond the scope of this book. However, one tool that has been useful for hundreds of organizations—in both the public and private sectors—over the past two decades is the strategy map. Robert Kaplan and David Norton developed this tool to help organizations determine the paths they could take to create sustainable value.[4] The map illustrates how an organization creates value by highlighting four perspectives: financial, customer, internal/operational, and learning and growth.

The *financial perspective* describes the tangible outcomes of a strategy in traditional financial terms (such as ROI, shareholder value, profitability, revenue growth, and lower unit costs). The *customer perspective* defines the value proposition the organization intends to use to generate sales and loyalty from targeted customers. (T. J. Maxx strategized that African American customers would value holiday ornaments that reflected their culture and race.) The *internal process perspective* identifies the critical processes for creating and delivering the customer value proposition. (In order for T. J. Maxx to stock the ornaments, they had to develop a supply chain that could provide the product.) Finally, the *learning and growth perspective* identifies how people, information systems, and organizational culture are managed to support those essential internal processes.[5] The strategy map comes to life when leaders work together to explore how the four perspectives connect to help the organization deliver on its mission and goals.

Strategy mapping is powerful because it is one way that leaders can grasp their organizational strategy and, from there, seek out relevant differences. It helps them to understand how different parts of the enterprise are interrelated and interdependent. It provides stakeholders a way of examining how they coordinate with one another and where there are gaps in their collaborations. And it reminds leaders that the search for relevant difference does not end with securing the representation of different types of people in the organization. Difference can also be relevant in how people come together to design and execute on internal processes, in understanding what matters to different segments of customers, and in managing shareholders and other stakeholders interested in bottom-line performance (for example, governments, regulatory agencies, and community organizations). When leaders ask themselves "what difference makes a difference," they have a broader set of options upon which to reflect. Strategy provides leaders with the canvas upon which to paint. But how do they actually choose the colors?

### *Always Assume That Difference Matters*

It's easier to see difference when you're looking for it. One simple step leaders can take to increase their capacity to see difference is to shift from trying to *ignore* difference to actually looking for it. In chapter 2, I discussed the importance of a leader's mindset toward difference and how it affects the ability of the leader to leverage difference. Assuming that difference is always present and potentially relevant frees a leader to explore differences that may not be immediately evident. To practice this skill at the personal level, you could approach a new acquaintance with the intent to explore how that person is unique or different from yourself. The interaction would become one of exploration and learning about a novel set of perspectives and experiences.

This approach is in direct contrast to approaches that seek to homogenize people. For example, in Europe many companies traditionally have taken diversity for granted and have spent decades fighting it by streamlining and integrating European supply systems. This has created a pervasive strategy of seeking to minimize differences between European markets and business locations.[6] In the United States, the common assertion that "I don't see color" captures this mindset. The statement reflects an ethos of *not* attending to difference—even though the difference does indeed exist. Unlike this "blindness" mindset, a "seeing" mindset incorporates the notion that every person holds diverse and possibly divergent perspectives from one's own, and that there is something to be learned from those perspectives.

Jerry Stenson,* the chief marketing officer of a U.S. national retail chain, described his evolving shift to a "difference matters" stance:

> I always believed that being fair meant treating people the same, giving them the same shot.... I saw all the quotas and the programs and I thought, "That's not right; that's not the fair way to operate." My good friend ... who is African American, we had

> some long conversations about this topic and it was really helpful for me.... I realized this point that being colorblind wasn't necessarily the best way to go at this. He was telling me that not seeing him as an African American was taking something away. I had never thought of it that way.

Of course, the moment of revelation is just the beginning. Assuming that difference does matter leads to behaviors that help to surface previously unseen differences. The core question becomes, What difference could be important in this setting or domain? Keeping in mind that leaders and stakeholders must reflect on their organizational strategy, a host of possible questions emerge: What differences in customer segments might be important? How can difference of perspective or skill set help us to improve this business process? What talents might my colleague have that can contribute to our team?

All these questions are geared toward naming the differences that may be relevant and worth exploring. They also challenge the questioner to be a detective and to search for differences that may not be obvious. None may surface immediately, but the questioning process may ultimately yield new ideas. Once leaders make this mindset shift, they need to make a habit of asking themselves—and their colleagues—what differences might be affecting the situation at hand. This shift in openness to difference is what encourages broader "seeing."

### *Manage Barriers to Seeing Clearly*

No matter how aware of strategy a leader is, or how open to learning about difference, blind spots that prevent him or her from seeing relevant differences are always present.

***Habits of Not Attending to Difference.*** The most pervasive cause of these blind spots in identifying difference is that leaders may not be accustomed to paying attention to differences. One reason is the strong cultural and historical legacy of the regimented, chain-of-command organizational structures that persist. With the Industrial Revolution's emphasis on product and process standardization, finding ways to make people and processes the same became a priority.[7] Of course, the Information Age has ushered in a variety of ways of organizing, but many leaders continue to structure their organizations—both consciously and unconsciously—in ways that value sameness. Given this background, leaders and other stakeholders have to work against "muscle memory" if they wish to cultivate a practice of highlighting difference.

A second factor that is especially powerful for U.S. leaders is the strong value placed on the idea that all people are equal, a belief that is grounded in the country's founding philosophy and documents. The nation's historical journey has involved the ongoing dilemma of dealing with the many ways this core belief has been compromised. Mistreatment of indigenous people, women, new immigrants, and Africans and their descendants—among others—has frequently called into question the integrity of our core national values. We met the challenge with perhaps the greatest resolve with the Civil Rights Movement of the mid-twentieth century. To eliminate the contradiction between the belief that people are equal and the legal, political, and social reality that black people were second-class citizens, many citizens adopted the attitude that our institutions must ignore the differences in others. This "colorblind" stance would hold that African Americans or women should not be forced to bear racial or gender labels: true equality would come from ignoring the labels and seeing another as just a person. That way, it becomes unacceptable to treat someone as anything less than a human being. This was a noble and groundbreaking stance. In the context of oppressive conditions like forced segregation, colorblindness was a way of revisioning society.

But in the diverse and global twenty-first century, the habit of colorblindness is debilitating. Consider the case of Diacom, Inc.,* where it caused significant problems. Diacom manufactured and maintained military ships and submarines, and the leaders of its research and development department struggled with job-specific differences and the tension around the status accompanying them. PhD scientists were at odds with non-PhD researchers, and employees with military backgrounds frequently clashed with non-military employees.

I began my work with Diacom by interviewing two relatively senior managers of the company. We sat together at a table as they spoke at some length about the PhD and military dynamics. PhD scientists' privilege relative to other researchers was analogous to what is seen in medical settings, where doctors have a high status relative to nurses and medical technicians. This made it quite challenging for the two groups to collaborate smoothly on teams. The military/nonmilitary tensions were evident in leadership styles. Military managers, relying on their training and experience, tended to use command-and-control techniques of management. Nonmilitary managers used a variety of styles, but were generally more comfortable with low-status-difference, collaborative styles of management. The military employees found the nonmilitary employees lax as managers, and the nonmilitary managers found their counterparts rigid and lacking in managerial competency.

As the conversation unfolded the two managers agreed with one another and jointly shared these perspectives. Before I ended the conversation, I asked the two if there were other tensions that were important at Diacom, and they agreed that we had covered the major ones. I then asked if gender or race were important, to which one of them, a black woman, responded, "Oh, of course that [gender] is an issue." She proceeded to speak about the challenges women faced in the company. Her white male colleague also elaborated on some of the challenges he saw his female colleagues experience. "But," they said, "we don't really talk about that at Diacom."

This dual consciousness is not uncommon. Differences are known (at least by some people) but not spoken about openly. They are only discussed if there is a safe context in which to do so. In one institution that had been sued for gender discrimination, whenever the topic of gender arose employees simply refused to discuss the issue. In most cases there was simply silence; at other times, people changed the topic. Avoiding certain differences because people are fearful of engaging in discussions about them is one way that difference is suppressed.

The Diacom employees claimed that race and gender were not issues any longer, that they were much less important than the PhD and military issues. But closer examination showed gender issues to be evident in ways that affected both women and men at Diacom.

First, they did business with the U.S. government, so they had to pay attention to certain differences in talent management to comply with government regulation. Second, my conversation with the two managers was repeated frequently with other Diacom employees, who spoke first about PhD and military tensions and then elaborated quite deeply on the "non-issues" of race and gender. In a couple of subsequent conversations, generational difference emerged as critical, too. Finally, I worked with a group of forty senior managers focused on strategy and difference. This group of white men and women talked for three hours with great energy and thoughtfulness about race and gender in their professional and personal lives.

Gender differences *were* relevant at Diacom—it was just hard for employees to overcome their habit of not paying attention to them. This lack of attention has a peculiar quality to it. Many people, especially those who are members of a lower status group (here, women), will certainly notice and discuss these issues privately. We know that in a group or an organization, the qualities that make you a minority stand out.[8] For example, a woman in a group of men is distinctive by virtue of her sex. Whenever possible, she will try to identify other women in the group, either to connect with them or to distance herself from them. If her goal is to connect, she and her female colleagues will likely talk about their experiences in the organization and discuss gender in those conversations; they are well aware of the dynamics and are seeking to make sense of them.

Yet they cultivate the habit of ignoring the difference when they are among colleagues from higher status groups (men in this example). Bringing differences to light evokes the fear that majority members will judge and reject them professionally and socially. At best, it stokes a culture of uneasiness and potential conflict as people struggle to know how to speak skillfully about the subject. At worst, speaking about difference becomes career-threatening. So members of the lower status groups put their heads down and try to simply focus on the work.

Majority members also develop a habit of ignoring the difference, but for other reasons. Most apparent is fear that highlighting a sensitive difference with a misspoken word or phrase can be career-limiting. The existence of civil rights regulations in many countries makes these offenses costly because they expose organizations to lawsuits. As a result, suspected offenders, predominantly majority-group individuals, are punished swiftly. It is easier to shut up than to risk sanction.

This anxiety is compounded by the psychological risk of noticing difference. We are all generally motivated to see ourselves as good people; we create positive and flattering images of ourselves to help others to see us in a positive light, and because it makes us feel good.[9] For majority members, being oblivious to differences can be a way to protect their positive self-image as a fair and just person. A white person can't be guilty of racism toward a black person if the white person never even noticed race. So it becomes important for the white person to *actively ignore* race.[10]

Protecting our positive self-images is no small issue. When we feel good about ourselves we perform better, individually and in collaboration with others.[11] And research on the effect of engaging in activities that threaten our positive self-image tells us that we prefer not to do that kind of thing.[12] For majority members, talking about difference—especially emotionally charged differences—makes it likely that majority members will end up feeling worse about themselves than when the conversation began. It is therefore easier for them to remain silent—and their remaining silent over a long period of time reinforces the habit of simply not seeing difference.

This obliviousness to difference only persists in an organization if high and low status members collude in not paying attention. Low status members keep their heads down and ignore difference with their high status colleagues and high status colleagues ignore difference as a way of managing felt risk. Soon people in the organization learn to enter into conversations like the one I had with the Diacom managers. If no one raises the issue of difference, it never comes up.

A great deal of subtlety and complexity are involved in *not* seeing difference. People in organizations are motivated consciously and unconsciously to limit their own perception of others' talents and personal resources. Learning to become a Leveraging Difference organization means ridding oneself and one's organization of the habit of narrowing what differences are seen.

***Eclipsed Difference.*** Relevant differences are often made invisible—or eclipsed—by an overemphasis on one difference to the exclusion of others. In the United States, this often occurs when race or gender or another highly charged difference so dominates the diversity discourse that other differences become invisible.

That is what happened at Washington Computing,* a large international technology company. The leaders of one of its divisions wanted to increase the representation of African Americans at their site. Other divisions had adopted this as a goal, and corporate headquarters touted the importance of minority representation in the company. The challenge was that this division was located in a sparsely populated, predominantly white rural part of the Pacific Northwest. The population of African Americans was negligible. As it turned out, these leaders had set the goal of increasing black representation because they had heard that sister divisions were making progress with this initiative. They assumed they could do the same.

Despite their enthusiasm, it was apparent that as long as the division was located at this site, they were never going to get black people to come there. The reason was simple—the site was just too remote and the population of African Americans too small. There was no cultural draw for black people, and even if the company had been willing to pay them a premium in compensation, that would have been, in a nutshell, a dumb move. This was no indictment of the division, nor was it a slight toward the community. Some people prefer to live and work in some places and not in other places. And it's not easy to change that fact.

But here is where the eclipse took place. The division needed to maintain a strong core capability in engineering research and development, the bread and butter of their business. They were drawing heavily on a talent pool of Asian American and Indian national engineers. They had been able to successfully attract these engineers, but they were experiencing rapid turnover, significantly greater than the industry average. Asked why they weren't focusing their diversity efforts on these engineers, one leader remarked that this was "not a diversity issue."

The problems didn't stop there. The division included nearly equal numbers of women and men, a few more men than women. But while men were distributed throughout all job levels, from top leadership to rank-and-file positions, most of the women were in the lower levels of the division hierarchy. There were no diversity initiatives in place to deal with gender. Several of the women voiced their concern, confidentially, about how difficult it was to advance, but it was unclear whether that concern was being effectively communicated to the male leaders.

This example illustrates some of the quandaries involved in seeing relevant differences within an organization. In this situation, divisional leadership was focused on addressing a difference that seemed to have importance. But the perception of importance was really being fueled by what other divisions were doing under the label of diversity management. Because the leaders were fixated on dealing with racial diversity (particularly black–white representation), they weren't paying close attention to more urgent diversity issues. They failed to see the attrition of foreign national engineers as "diversity critical." They seemed oblivious to the fact that there was dissatisfaction among talented women in the division, and that those women's skills were underutilized. And they hadn't even begun to spot the other kinds of differences, in addition to culture and gender, that could have been affecting the division in critical ways.

Eclipses of relevant differences like the ones at Washington Computing occur frequently in organizations, for many reasons. One difference may outshine others because making progress seems more possible in that area than in the others. Or one difference dominates because a crisis such as a lawsuit looms, so that issue consumes the organization's attention and resources. Indeed, for some organizations crisis mode becomes their modus operandi as they proceed from year to year, focusing on the difference for which they feel the greatest external pressure to respond. In each of these cases, organizations and leaders ignore or minimize important differences because their view is obscured by other differences.

***Undercover Difference.*** Relevant differences are also hard to identify because those who possess the differences may choose to hide them. A highly creative manager who naturally thinks "outside the box" may spend a good deal of time working on being more linear and logical with her linear-thinking colleagues. Because she wants to fit in with the team, she downplays her creative thinking skills so that she looks more like her colleagues. Of course, the team suffers as a result because it loses her ability to deal innovatively with problems. An even more pervasive example of "undercover difference" is the gay manager who chooses not to reveal his sexual orientation even though it could be the source of important new perspectives and relevant resources.

These examples differ in how the two managers are likely to assess the risk involved in sharing their difference. If the creative manager reveals her different way of thinking, she may seem odd, but she will likely continue to be embraced and included as a colleague. The gay manager who comes out risks experiencing subtle exclusions by his heterosexual colleagues—especially other males—who struggle to manage their discomfort over dealing with a gay colleague. In more extreme situations—which still exist—the gay manager could face overt discrimination and physical intimidation. The important point is simply that people have a myriad of motivations for not revealing differences that could very well be important in creating value for an organization.

*Distorted Difference.* Leaders and organizations also fail to see relevant differences because their view of a particular difference is distorted: it is though they are wearing a pair of glasses with an outdated prescription. In other words, difference is missed or ignored because of bias. Few words are as loaded when talking about diversity and difference as this one. One reason is that bias has spawned insidious forms of discrimination and oppression affecting people all over the world. Racism, sexism, and other systemic discrimination are rooted in unfair and ultimately illegitimate biases.

But with new research, we are learning that the ways bias affects our perceptions is even more nuanced than we thought. For a long time, we assumed that people who were prejudiced toward others were conscious of their biases and fundamentally *chose* to be prejudiced (or at least chose not to change their attitude). However, research over the past three decades is making the unassailable case that not all bias is intentional or under the control of the biased person.[13] Psychologists Anthony Greenwald, Brian Nosek, Mahzarin Banaji, and their colleagues have shown that some bias is clearly not conscious.

Implicit associations and implicit biases shape our behavior in ways that surprise us and even shock us once we see them.[14] Our perception is "guided" by social and psychological forces that often we are not even aware of. For example, Malcolm Gladwell, in his best-selling book *Blink*, describes how the perception of height in men creates surprising (or not so surprising) outcomes. The average height of a U.S. male is five feet nine inches tall. But when Gladwell collected data on Fortune 500 CEOs, he discovered that they averaged just less than six feet in height. And there is more: even though only about 14.5 percent of U.S. men are six feet or taller, 58 percent of these CEOs fall into that category.[15] These findings suggest that tall men are perceived as capable corporate leaders, but shorter men seem less like "CEO material."

It is unlikely that decision-makers sit back and say, "How tall is candidate X? Under six feet? I don't know if this will work." It is much more plausible that they are simply trying to make what they believe are informed decisions, and the resulting height pattern is the product of unconscious bias. Why this happens is certainly interesting, but of greater importance is the pivotal question the data lead us to ask: Are taller people better than shorter people as leaders of corporations in the twenty-first century? If so, then corporations would do well to include height in their senior executive job descriptions. If not, we are seeing a bias-driven blind spot in action.

Height isn't the only dimension along which bias creates blind spots. In a study exploring attitudes about weight, researchers asked 101 students to make a series of choices between prospective teammates in a trivia contest in which the winner got a cash prize. Possible teammates varied on three dimensions relevant to performance in the contest (education, IQ, experience) and one dimension that was irrelevant (body weight). The students were given factual information on the three relevant dimensions, and to convey body weight they were shown photographs of male and female teammate candidates in which the same face was manipulated to appear either thin or overweight. Although the students stated explicitly that weight had little impact on their decisions, in fact it mattered quite a bit. Weight was a more likely predictor of who would be chosen than any other factor even though weight was irrelevant to performance. Indeed, participants were essentially willing to trade an overweight teammate with an IQ of 101 for a thin teammate with an IQ of 90.[16]

These examples reveal that relevant difference can be missed because our instruments for seeing difference may be compromised. Research tells us that our instruments are inevitably flawed and that we will always be vulnerable to distortions in the way we perceive difference. As a result, the differences that look to us at first glance like the most important ones actually may not be.

### *Make Connections*

Managing barriers to seeing difference is essential. Another powerful way to enhance the ability to see is by making connections with others. This can be done in professional or personal contexts, and the connections may be brief or long standing. The key is that they help sharpen your lens for seeing difference.

***Be Open to Different People.*** Over fifty years of social psychological research confirms the intuitive notion that bringing together people who are different can reduce prejudice and stereotypical thinking.[17] This classic "contact hypothesis" research reinforces the fact that under the right conditions the more people who are different get to know one another, the better their chances of getting along.[18] But exposure has another effect: the more we are exposed to differences, the more those differences become familiar. Nuance and detail become more evident.

By studying the effect that exposure has on focus, Steven Young and Heather Claypool found that when someone is exposed to a novel stimulus—a colleague of difference, for example—two things happen. If the person has a bias against the difference the colleague embodies, repeated exposure softens the bias. And more exposure to people with that difference increases positive feelings about them, which in turn increases the attention paid to them.[19] What this means is that exposure to people who are different encourages us to feel less afraid and more open to them, and to pay more attention to their appearance, dress, mannerisms, and various other subtle cues.

I've experienced this firsthand. When I was younger, I was not tuned in to ethnic differences. This is ironic, given the ethnic diversity in my hometown of Cleveland, Ohio. I grew up on the east side of the city on Eddy Road. My neighborhood was exclusively black. and all my friends who lived near me were black. Of course, I knew there were white people in Cleveland and in the world. I watched TV, and we traveled freely through much of the predominantly white city (though I did pick up at an early age that—true or not—it was unsafe to travel through "Little Italy," or too far to the west side of the city). Attending public school was my first close interaction with white children my age. And when all was said and done, I could look them all over and think to myself, "Yup, they're all just white." My problem was that I couldn't see beyond the large and imprecise category of just being white.

With greater exposure, though, I began to see more. I attended a predominantly white high school and spent much more time with a variety of white kids. I started to see that there were varieties of white people, not just one generic brand. I began to notice differences in skin tone and in combinations of skin and hair color. I noticed subtle differences in accents among different friends (despite our common Ohio dialect). My Anglo white friends had different facial features than my Jewish friends. Both groups differed from my friends of Eastern European descent. My lens for seeing white people became much more precise as a result of my increased exposure. I began to see difference that I had been unable to see before.

This sharpening of the lens for seeing more subtle cues has secondary benefits. Leaders begin to put two and two together. They begin to note that the dark-skinned colleague who looks like an African American but is wearing a Hindu Durga necklace may be of African descent but not be from the United States. And upon hearing her proper British accent, they may gain further insight about her nationality (U.K., or British colony?) and educational background. To the unattuned leader, this colleague might simply look African American—a conclusion that has implications for how she is approached as a person and as a resource for the organization. But to the leader with a refined lens for seeing difference, she will bring a very different array of possible resources and experiences. It's all in the seeing.

One last benefit of greater exposure to people who are different is the likelihood of seeing more examples of diverse people doing different kinds of work. One contributor to bias, both implicit and explicit, is role slotting.[20] Women frequently end up in HR jobs (because they are "great with people"), Asians are hired for technical jobs (because they are "great with numbers"), and so on. With a larger pool of people who are visibly different performing in a variety of non-stereotypical jobs, it is harder to maintain these stereotypes. This helps diminish distortion in our seeing.[21]

At New Frontiers Financial Services, CEO James Dormand* made a point of meeting with employee resource groups (ERGs) on a quarterly basis. In this organization, the primary ERGs were for women, Hispanics, gays and lesbians, and African Americans. Often these were lunch meetings in which the CEO met with group members to talk about what they saw as critical issues within the organization. These meetings had two positive effects. They demonstrated that he had interest in and commitment to a better understanding of ERG members' experiences. And they sharpened the CEO's lens for seeing difference. As he sat in the room with his Hispanic employees, Dormand realized that he was rarely in the same space as so many Hispanics. He noted that before the meeting began people spoke in combinations of English, Spanish, and Spanglish. Because this ERG included managers and staff, he saw people who worked in office spaces that he never visited. He saw how executives and lower-level employees struggled to interact. He noted the ways in which people looked different and began to compare and contrast Hispanics of Mexican, Cuban, and Puerto Rican descent.

What he learned in ongoing conversations with ERG members was powerful, of course. In terms of the Leveraging Difference Cycle, these meetings increased his capacity for understanding difference. But simply committing to being in the room is what helped him see difference more powerfully.

***Engage Insiders.*** The premise behind exposing oneself to difference is that one learns to see more by connecting with the unfamiliar. But another way to see difference is to engage with "insiders." By contrast, insiders are the mainstream members of the organization. They are usually the majority and usually have a more monolithic identity. In the U.S., insiders are usually heterosexual white men. It's easy to understand how engaging outsiders—people who are different from the norm—can lead to seeing new differences. But engaging insiders also surfaces differences. I frequently ask groups of insiders to talk about what differences matter to them in how they do their work. They are often surprised at the question and pause before speaking. When they start talking, it is sometimes hard to write everything down, the ideas flow so quickly. They talk about learning styles, introversion and extroversion, aggressiveness, and a host of other topics.

My colleagues and I worked with the leadership team at a second division of the Delvin Mining Corporation. The team was made up of seven white men, and we helped them develop skills to manage conflict within the unit. During a break, one team member walked up to me and said, "You know I'm the nigger of this group." He caught me completely off guard. I didn't know if he was trying to be funny, insulting, or serious. I learned quickly that he was very serious. He explained that as an Italian American member of an Anglo American team, he was frequently singled out, ridiculed (all in good fun, of course), and limited in opportunities for advancement. He also noted that he was short, olive-skinned, and balding among a group of tall, fair-skinned men with full heads of hair. These differences mattered deeply to this man, and probably to others like him. But they were much less obvious than what we usually see as difference.

A leader can foster such conversations and benefit from them. Engaging with insiders can help a leader gain awareness of how people in the organization are seeing the differences in their worlds. And the leader—who is usually the ultimate insider—may gain greater *self-awareness* about his own differences and how they may be affecting his leadership. Seeing more kinds of difference in the organization is certainly valuable—that is a core takeaway from this chapter. And when a leader sees new differences within himself, he teaches others to explore and see differences in themselves and in the larger organization.

## Conclusion: What's the Difference?

The ability to leverage difference starts with being open to potentially relevant differences. The practice of seeing difference in the first place creates grist for the mill. But in a hypercompetitive, complex world, leaders and organizations can be bombarded by all kinds of variations among people: differences in experience, skill, opinions, perspectives, professional maturity, and on and on. Seeing difference *well* is the activity of identifying which variations are relevant and important to the organization and bringing them to the surface. And as we have seen, a host of challenges makes it all the more difficult to sort out which differences matter and which ones don't. The dilemma is captured in this Seeing Difference Matrix:

**Figure 3 The Seeing Difference Matrix**

| | Strategically Relevant | Not Strategically Relevant |
|---|---|---|
| **Attend to Difference** | Ready to continue on Leveraging Difference Cycle | Diversion |
| **Ignore Difference** | Opportunity cost | |

The sweet spot is the upper lefthand quadrant. Here leaders are attending to strategically relevant differences and are poised to continue on through the Leveraging Difference Cycle. They run into problems when they land in either the upper right or lower left quadrants. Ignoring differences that are strategically relevant (the lower left quadrant) keeps them invisible in the organization and thus unavailable to be capitalized upon. Moreover, missing relevant differences discourages and demoralizes those who possess them; the difference is invisible to the organization and, as was true for Adriana, individuals come to *feel* like they are invisible in the organization.

But organizations also run into trouble when they focus on differences that simply aren't relevant. Washington Computing's problems illustrate how focusing on an irrelevant difference diverts organizations from focusing on the really critical, really important differences. Doing so deprives leaders of the chance both to solve problems and exploit opportunities resulting from those differences.

Ultimately, leaders want to attend to the relevant differences in their organizations. If they can do that, they are ready to move to the next step in the Leveraging Difference Cycle—*understanding difference.*

## Key Takeaways

1. Seeing difference is the act of identifying the differences that are strategically important for an organization.
2. The costs of not attending to relevant difference range from missing critical opportunities to excel to leaving valuable employees disenfranchised and disengaged.
3. These skills are needed to see difference:

    - Understanding the strategy for your enterprise. Tools like strategy mapping can be helpful in creating consensus on strategic priorities.
    - Assuming that difference will matter in any business situation and that seeing it could lead to benefits.
    - Managing the barriers that prevent seeing difference: not paying attention, eclipsed difference, concealed difference, distorted difference.
    - Making connections, with different others and with insiders.

# 5

# Understanding Difference

Understanding difference is the capacity to gather and integrate comprehensive and accurate knowledge about relevant differences so that the organization can successfully leverage them. This learning process is essential, because by definition the introduction of difference is the introduction of that which is new and unknown to the organization. Focusing on difference is thus an opportunity for innovation and change, but attempts to engage and leverage differences usually don't work if these differences are not well understood.

Consider the case of Aeolian Accounting in chapter 1. CEO Alan Jerrold had made an unsuccessful push to hire women associates in the hope of gaining more female partners over time. His leadership team was worried that they weren't getting access to the entire talent pool relative to their competitors, and they really believed it would be good to have more women within their ranks—though they weren't especially articulate about why. They tried to make the change but failed at the execution stage. Aeolian had leapt to the step of hiring the women immediately, assuming that their mere presence would somehow produce the conditions for success, both for the women recruits and for the firm. What they missed, though, was any thorough understanding about women and about Aeolian itself. Senior leaders clung to the notion that these female accounting professionals were no different from the men in the same profession. In fact, they genuinely believed that assuming that there were any significant differences would be insulting to the women.

As a result, it never occurred to them that they should study the experiences of women in the industry to better understand what these new colleagues might encounter. For example, they didn't know about an American Institute of Certified Public Accountants (AICPA) survey conducted among more than 20,000 accounting professionals. That research revealed that only 41 percent of senior women managers aspired to be partners, compared to 65 percent of men managers—and that aspirational gap widened the further down the hierarchy you looked. Aeolian leaders also didn't realize how important it was for the women in the firm to have effective mentoring experiences and to see female role models. And they didn't grasp the disadvantages women would face because of gender stereotyping.[1]

Furthermore, Aeolian leaders didn't fully grasp the strategic benefit they would receive from having more women. Company strategy emphasized the development and leveraging of relationships and social networks. This was critical for marketing the firm's services, building strong client relationships, and insuring high performance by its global teams. Having women in leadership roles as well as in key functional areas could provide a distinct competitive advantage. Women have been shown, in general, to have a more participative and less directive leadership style than men, some-

**Figure 4 Understanding Difference**

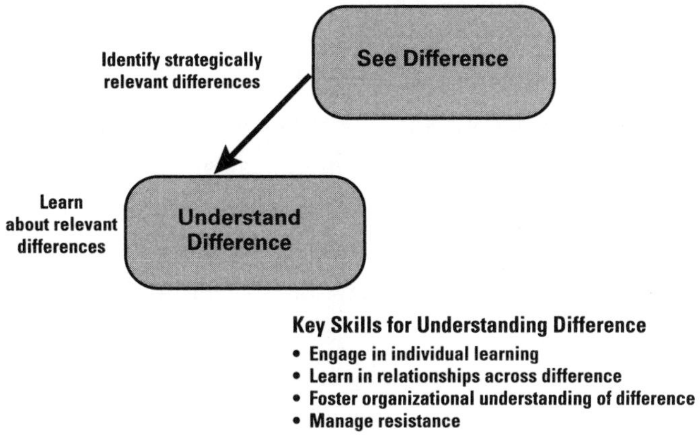


thing that could enhance collaboration and team performance.[2] Finally, having more women could provide a context for learning how to create a more inclusive and flexible company culture, with more ways to establish and sustain a work–life balance and at the same time enhance performance.

Without these insights about who women were and how they mattered strategically, Aeolian was slow to create the kind of environment in which women could thrive. Though flex-time arrangements were put into place, there remained a stigma around taking advantage of the option; those who did so were seen as less reliable. Aeolian's leaders did not really understand the experiences of the women they were recruiting, as they did not understand how having women fully integrated into the firm could further its strategic goals.

All too often, leaders and organizations see difference and attempt to leverage it without first educating themselves. They frequently assume that new people brought into the organization will figure out how to be effective in the same way that everyone else did. But this is an untenable assumption. And when it comes to differences in customer perspective, assumptions like this can lead to disappointing results in gaining market share.

Even attempts to incorporate difference into internal processes can go awry if rigorous learning hasn't taken place. Kulick & Soffa, a manufacturer of semiconductor assembly equipment, was looking to achieve growth in its wire bonding tools segment—in particular, capillaries and dicing saw blades—through geographic expansion and entry into new markets.

In 2002 it manufactured the capillaries in Yokneam, Israel, and the blades in Santa Clara, California. Its leadership team, mindful of the substantial expense involved in maintaining two sites, had been charged with consolidating operations and designing and opening a single new facility in Suzhou, China. To make a wise move, they needed to understand both the cultural trade-offs between operating in Israel and China, as well as the technical trade-offs. Their final decision to move to Suzhou took into account differences in the age of the labor force, turnover, and policies about intellectual property in China, to name but a few of the key issues they needed to consider.[3]

## How to Understand Difference

Leaders promote understanding about relevant difference by building—and supporting their people in building—competencies in four activity domains: individual learning, leveraging relationships across differences, having in place organizational systems for understanding difference, and managing resistance to understanding difference.

### *Engage in Individual Learning*

*Be Curious.* One of the most important building blocks for understanding difference is the desire to learn about difference. This curiosity about differences provides the motivation to engage in the activities that actually enhance learning. People vary in how curious they are in general. Those who have a high curiosity level actively seek out and thoroughly process information in many areas. Those low in curiosity rely more on simple cues, cognitive heuristics, and stereotypes in interpreting situations and judging people.[4] Obviously, being more curious fuels greater understanding of difference.

Gerald Ames, a senior executive from Diacom, exemplified the highly curious individual. Ames was a white male, born and raised in the suburbs of Washington, D.C. He was extremely interested in culture and ethnicity, and he was energetic—almost aggressive—in his questioning about what was going on in his company. He described how few candidates of color to whom they had offered positions had accepted the offers. He wanted to learn why, and he wanted to understand why the employees of color who did come were so dissatisfied. But his interest was not confined to company issues. He and I sat together at dinner one evening after I had worked with a group of high-potential managers in his company. He peppered me with questions, eagerly exploring the implications of a Barack Obama presidency (Obama had just been elected). How was the president-elect being perceived in black communities, relative to white communities? Was there uniform support, or was there friction? How would the president's race affect his ability to lead globally? After we had talked for an hour, I asked Ames why he was so interested in all of this. "I don't know," he said. "I just want to learn about this stuff!"

Becoming curious requires a foundation of basic knowledge about a particular difference—"seed" information—that captures a person's attention. Curiosity is difficult to muster without this.[5] Seed information comes from reading books and magazines, attending films or plays, or regularly scanning such sources of information as newsletters or web home pages. Having a variety of communications media within an organization—newsletters, art exhibits, etc.—can be effective providers of seed information.

This seed information is the most effective when it is about some aspect of difference that's personally and emotionally relevant. As it turned out, Ames had had a series of important professional and personal relationships with African Americans dating back to childhood. Those relationships had been the source of both enjoyment and regrets, feelings that motivated him to want to learn more. Finding these emotional "hooks" for oneself through reflection and conversation can illuminate a path for stimulating curiosity about difference.

Curiosity about difference is also encouraged when people become aware of a gap between what they know and what they think they know. Curiosity is frequently squelched when people are unaware of what they don't know, whether it's from lack of information and experience, overconfidence, dogmatism, or simple arrogance. Curiosity diminishes when anyone settles into the attitude that there is little else to learn. To combat this, the key is making gaps visible in a manageable way. Providing seed information or offering interpersonal feedback are two ways to do so. Self-awareness, in turn, can enhance curiosity.[6] One caution about exposing blind spots: feedback can't be too threatening, or the person is likely to disengage. When a trusted colleague privately told me that I was consistently behaving rudely toward a female colleague, I was embarrassed and decided to change the behavior and understand why I was doing it. Had that colleague reported me to the ombudsperson, I doubt if curiosity would have been the first thing to come to my mind.

Curiosity is fostered by a combination of incentives to learn mixed with the autonomy to decide how to learn. External motivators can foster curiosity, but nobody can be forced to be curious. Rather, leaders and organizations can create a context in which learning is an attractive option. The employees of one division of Allerton Consulting, a medium-sized management consulting firm, began the practice of monthly "Global Lunches." The idea was to help colleagues better understand the global markets in which they were operating as well as some of the emerging markets they planned to move into. Allerton had a strong representation of managers and associates from outside the United States, and it had a very collegial culture. A group of employees came up with the idea of lunches at which a particular country or culture was featured. Cuisine from the focus culture was featured, and employees led spirited discussions about the country and culture.

The Global Lunches were always well attended and lively. Employees commented that they were terrific venues for learning about cultural differences and for stoking curiosity. They seemed to be effective for a combination of reasons. Allerton had people from different cultures already embedded in the organization: about 25 percent of the employees were from outside the U.S. The firm's collegial culture made it appealing to learn about these colleagues; people were interested in those with whom they worked. And attendance was purely voluntary—only people who wanted to attend showed up. But the positive experience that spread from the events drew more and more employees. The curiosity was contagious.

*Do Research.* The most powerful method of gaining understanding is to gather information. One way to do so is through the cognitive learning that occurs by being exposed to information about difference. Exposure to news and current events, literature, films, and Internet sources can provide leaders and organizations with a continuous flow of information about differences.

These data sources need not be limited to passive modes of learning. Individuals can seek out events and experiences that take place where difference arises. In many organizations, managers arrange regular outings to cultural festivals in the local community as a way to expose themselves and their colleagues to cultural differences that characterize their customer base. At Credit Suisse in New York, the Diversity for the Americas team regularly gathered books and magazines about current issues around the globe. They made these available not just in designated diversity libraries but also in offices, reception areas, and leisure spaces throughout the firm.

All the activities discussed so far—cultivating curiosity, seeking out resources, and exposing oneself to experiences—can be self-motivated. Doing them in collaboration with others is often equally or even more powerful. But anyone who chooses to build competency in understanding difference can begin on their own without delay.

### *Learn in Relationships across Differences*

The full power of differences in organizations unfolds in relationships between people across differences. That makes professional and personal relationships extremely fertile grounds for understanding difference. Yet it can be extremely challenging to cultivate those relationships in ways that promote deep understanding and ultimately help create the capability for leveraging difference in an organization. The case of Braylon Foster* and Erik Harmon* illustrates some of the dilemmas in cross-difference relationships.

Foster wasn't quite sure how to manage his relationship with Harmon. The two were associates at Allerton Consulting and often ended up working on the same project team. Both were smart, well trained, and capable, and they complemented one another well. Foster was particularly skilled in client relationship management. An excellent "translator," he helped the team understand client needs, and he helped clients understand how the team worked. Harmon was an outstanding strategist with a keen understanding of how to address clients' strategic challenges.

The two frequently worked closely together and really "clicked." They had the same quirky sense of humor. But both realized there were tensions in the relationship: Foster was straight, Harmon openly gay. Foster became preoccupied with what he could or couldn't talk about with Harmon. Sometimes he felt uneasy about appearing too familiar with Harmon for fear that others would think he, too, was gay. From time to time, the problems Foster had in romantic relationships made him question his own sexuality. Why did he get along so well with Harmon?

From Harmon's view, Foster was clearly edgy when the two of them were working alone together, and this was starting to bother him. Harmon, unlike Foster, was in a committed relationship, and he and his partner were seriously considering marriage. Because he and Foster worked so closely together, he suspected that Foster, like so many straight men, was probably uneasy. Harmon was frustrated that all this was getting in the way of the great work that the two of them could accomplish when each was on his game.

Neither talked about their concerns. Foster was afraid that he would say something offensive or inappropriate, and that such a misstep could sour a good working relationship. Harmon was overcome with a sense of resignation that talking about this with Foster just wasn't worth it. He had tried to educate straight guys about this kind of thing before, and usually he was met with defensiveness and homophobia, subtle or overt.

The inability of these two men to deal with the tension around sexual orientation has quietly built a wedge between them. Since they work well together, each convinces himself that it is too risky to address the tension. They both fail to consider two important factors. First, they don't anticipate the potential impact of their mutual discomfort on the working relationship. Each acknowledges his own discomfort but is unable to fully understand and empathize with the other's concerns. This disconnect can erode a working relationship over time and diminish productivity.

Even more costly is the fact that their unwillingness to talk about the situation deprives them of an opportunity to learn about difference from one another. This is one of the most profound inhibitors to understanding: colleagues are afraid to learn together. What can individuals like Foster and Harmon do to change this pattern? How can people who are different make their relationship an ongoing laboratory for learning?

### *Four Skills That Support Relationships across Difference*

Engaging another individual across differences requires four core relational skills: inquiry, listening, self-disclosure, and managing feedback.

*Inquiry*—a skill motivated by curiosity—primarily means asking questions. By asking questions, a person gains understanding of the other person's perspective and acquires knowledge about that person.[7] But this skill goes deeper than simply acquiring information verbally. It extends to asking about the rationales that lead to the other's conclusions, and exploring assumptions about the other person's goals and interests.[8]

*Listening* is important in interpersonal interactions because it helps a person understand what another person is trying to communicate. It also provides an opportunity to elicit the maximum amount of relevant information during an interaction. But listening has long-term effects that are especially powerful in sustaining relationships across difference. The willingness to listen in the moment signals to the other person that you are interested in what he or she has to express. By conveying this genuine interest, the listener lays a foundation for trust and respect that carries over to future interactions. This mutual trust and respect bonds the two and eases the way when the relationship encounters the conflicts that are likely to emerge.

*Self-disclosure* is the act of sharing relevant information about oneself to the other person.[9] This can be done through description or, more powerfully, through personal narratives about one's own experiences involving the differences. If Foster and Harmon choose to strengthen their working relationship, for example, the ability of both men to talk about what it means and feels like to carry his sexual identity could be helpful to the other. But self-disclosure is also a dynamic process in which personal information and truths shift as two individuals are engaged in a relationship. To that end, it is important to share one's reactions with the other as they emerge in the relationship. For example, if an individual is annoyed by something the other person says, expressing the annoyance is an act of self-disclosure. These "real-time" disclosures are an essential aspect of openness in relationships across differences, because such relationships are so often shrouded in misunderstanding and mistrust. This kind of disclosure promotes transparency and counteracts the experiences of silence and subversion that commonly characterize these relationships.[10]

*Managing feedback*—the fourth basic skill—involves both giving and receiving feedback. Access to accurate feedback about professional and personal behavior is essential for fostering high performance at work and maintaining vibrancy and authenticity in a relationship. However, a lack of comfort and competence in building relationships across many differences (such as race, gender, and sexual orientation) can make it difficult to give and receive feedback.

This can manifest itself in two ways: biased feedback-givers may provide feedback that is simply inaccurate; or one party in a relationship may withhold constructive feedback for fear that it will dishearten the other or make the feedback-giver seem unsupportive or prejudiced. In either instance, the ability of both individuals to learn from one another is compromised. For effective learning in a relationship, there must be timely and frank exchange of behaviorally specific information, coupled with clear communication about the behavior's impact on task-focused and relationship-focused outcomes.

With these four basic skills in hand, dialogue across differences can happen in an atmosphere of openness and learning. Colleagues may talk about their differences because they are assigned to work together and want to perform well. Or they may talk simply to strengthen their relationship. Either way, they can act on their desire to learn and will be able to use their core skills to sustain the learning.

***The Advanced Skill: Manage Conflict across Difference***

Relationships across difference will engender conflict. Sometimes the conflict is overt. For example, a Sikh engineer is frustrated and offended when he is told by his supervisor to remove his *dastar* (the traditional turban required of baptized Sikhs) because "headwear is prohibited by company policy." Or the conflict may be more subtle, as in the case of a white male manager who fears he will be perceived as racist or sexist if he gives critical feedback to his Latina subordinate. In these examples, the actions and fears of one colleague create discord in the relationship. Even interactions that are initiated in the spirit of openness and learning can be perceived initially as threatening or offensive by the other party.

Understanding difference emerges when individuals engage with one another in constructive ways. Unfortunately, people typically have strong incentives to do just the opposite. They avoid talking with one another in these situations because they worry they will be punished for having such conversations. They are concerned, for example, that complaints will be filed against them if they inadvertently offend someone. And they may worry about the more subtle retribution of being ignored when advancement opportunities arise.

The core motivation for not talking about difference, however, is the fear that doing so is risky, even dangerous. A manager feels the risk of interacting in a domain in which he isn't very skilled, worrying that he might come off looking incompetent or, even worse, malevolent. Or he worries that he won't be able to deal appropriately with his anger or frustration over a colleague's remark. When a U.S. manager confused the names of two Chinese colleagues, the man being addressed felt demeaned by the name mixup and annoyed with his U.S. peer. When a male associate was chided by two female colleagues because he was "clueless about what women deal with," he felt embarrassed and resentful. These are examples of what Robin Ely, Debra Meyerson, and I coined "identity abrasions."[11] Identity abrasions are psychological "twinges" that one experiences when feeling put down or affronted—injuries to one's self-image. Such identity abrasions prompt a person to behave defensively at critical moments in a cross-difference relationship. And they encourage that person to see the other as the problem.

Identity abrasions can easily push two people apart from one another. People tend to do whatever it takes to bolster and protect their images of themselves as good, well-meaning individuals. One common response to identity abrasion is to disengage, undermining any opportunity to use the relationship to understand difference better.

Turning debilitating identity abrasions into powerful opportunities to understand difference requires enlisting any or all of five principles of behavior.[12] Each principle carries with it a set of skills an individual can use to execute on the principle. These key principles are:

- Pausing
- Connecting to larger goals
- Questioning your own role in the interaction
- Seeking out balanced support
- Shifting your mindset toward seeing opportunities

You can draw on these principles at many different points in a relationship, but they are especially powerful at times of conflict.

These principles aren't meant to be invoked in a sequential way, or necessarily all for a single incident. They can be called upon, sometimes simultaneously, throughout the learning process in a relationship. But together they contribute to your overall ability to manage identity abrasions constructively and create opportunities for understanding in the relationship.

***Pausing.*** Pausing means taking the time to identify feelings and consider the options that will help you to respond effectively in the face of identity abrasion. Pausing goes against the natural tendency to reactively feel and express anger, hurt, or blame—reactions that usually incite defensiveness in the other person, hinder the ability to learn, and fail to make us really feel much better. The core skill that supports the ability to pause is mindfulness, a receptive attention to and awareness of present events and experience.[13]

Pausing requires that a person be aware she or he is experiencing an identity abrasion, which in turn allows for short-circuiting the defensive reactions. Sam, a Jewish manager, was confronted at the year-end holiday party by a colleague who said he was "sick and tired of whitewashing Christmas because of all the other groups who might get offended." Sam was ready to lash back, but instead he chose to take several deep breaths and not confront his colleague at that moment. This prepared him to act on some of the other principles.

Just pausing seems like a simple action, but it can be extremely difficult in the heat of the moment. Sam paused by stopping his impulse to lash out, sitting quietly instead. There may be other behaviors that you might choose in order to pause. For example, one can practice simple mindfulness meditation, focusing on breathing or some other simple stimulus. This can reduce physiological reactivity and enhance the ability to regulate one's emotions.[14] It can also foster a greater sense of choice in one's behavioral responses.[15] Another strategy is the "self-talk"— engaging in an internal conversation about the situation. Observers wouldn't necessarily notice any significant behavioral change, but the affected individual would be engaged in rational-emotive reflection.[16] Finally, writing down reflections about the experience may help some people to begin to process their reactions.[17]

***Connecting to Larger Goals.*** The kind of moment Sam experienced, when unchecked, usually prompts us to focus inward on our own outrage and hurt. The first impulse is to burrow in and defend one's position. Connecting provides a way to resist this impulse by focusing outward on larger goals—such as contributing to a task, strengthening a team's dynamic, or fulfilling an organization's mission. Meaningful goals make it easier to remember why it is worth engaging with another, even as the experience is threatening in that moment.

In his reflective moment, Sam thought about what would be helpful to promote more powerful learning about religious sensitivity and what would help him to interact honestly and respectfully with his colleague. He also thought about what would help the firm be a more hospitable place for people of different faiths. The colleague who had made the remark was someone he had to work with closely in the coming weeks, and he wanted their working relationship to be a great one. Sam decided to talk with his colleague about the meaning of the Jewish holy days for him when he was a kid, and about his hope that there could be a way for everyone to feel that their traditions were respected at this time of the year. The discussion about Sam's own experience engaged his colleague, and they had a frank and powerful conversation about how people in the firm were treated.

That conversation happened because Sam was able to connect by asking himself some questions: What is most important, above and beyond my "attitude"? What would help my Jewish colleagues, and my colleagues of different faiths? What will help me be able to work well with this person? Questions like these help reframe a situation in a way that frees one from retreating into his or her own pain and frustration. And, by the way, doing so does *not* eliminate the opportunity for dealing fairly with an incivility or injustice that may have been the original source of the pain. Sam was hurt by the comment; it was a harmful act to him. Sometimes the appropriate response is clear feedback about the harm that has been done. But by connecting, Sam was afforded the choice of productive and creative ways to address that harmful act. He chose engagement.

***Questioning Yourself.*** The principle of questioning yourself is difficult because it requires examining how you might be contributing to your own identity abrasion! It requires asking yourself how the way you see the situation could be biased or distorted. And it calls into question the righteous indignation that often results when it appears that someone has behaved hurtfully toward you. The reason for this questioning is to come to a realistic and accurate understanding of what is transpiring in the relationship. It invites you to consider—not concede, but consider—that part of the responsibility for the negative interaction or relationship may rest with you.

Susan had been executive assistant to Priya for two years and was about to quit. She was fed up with Priya's autocratic behavior and dismissive style. Susan was extremely competent and had received feedback to that effect from her previous bosses. But Priya was constantly asking her to do more, and to do it more quickly. And when Susan met Priya's aggressive timelines, Priya rarely acknowledged that her efforts were noteworthy. Priya offered a quick "Great, thanks" and moved on to the next task.

Susan's initial reaction was that this Indian woman was just used to having servants at her beck and call. But realizing that she loved her work, Susan paused and tried to understand what was contributing to the tension she felt in relation to Priya. Motivated by the desire to make the situation better, Susan approached Priya to voice her concerns. She described her frustration, but chose not to blame Priya for making her feel that way. She asked how she could be helpful in a more satisfying way, expressing her desire to enjoy the working relationship more.

Priya immediately apologized and said she had not been aware of the impact her behavior was having. She shared that in her upbringing, she had worked with servants and was still in part operating from that mindset. Priya told Susan that she wanted to build a better working relationship and that she really valued Susan's efficiency. The relationship improved somewhat, and although Susan eventually moved to another position, the two became friends.

Susan's willingness to ask herself what she might have been contributing to the problem gave her the motivation and confidence to approach Priya directly to discuss the challenges they were facing. It also freed her from the self-righteous feeling that would have led her to blame Priya for the problems in their relationship. In conversations the two had over the several months before Susan moved, the two women shared stories and built an understanding about each other that illuminated their cultural, educational, and status experiences. This allowed them to fashion a stronger, more meaningful relationship and to collaborate better.

***Seeking Out Balanced Support.*** It isn't easy to undertake the steps to manage your reaction to conflict. Having support from others is essential, but having the right kind of support is what is most critical. Some friends and colleagues are great because they reinforce us, no matter what our behavior. They are our "puppy dog" friends, who show us their love and support with unconditional positive regard. They will even support us in denigrating someone we feel has wronged us.

These are not the friends we need in these situations. Instead, we need friends and colleagues who can help us sort through our abrasion reactions and connect with the larger goals. They question us and thereby help us question ourselves. Puppy dog support can feel good in the moment, but it is just the opposite of what we really need: the counsel of trusted colleagues who can help us see our choices about how to behave or what to believe, and point out alternatives.

***Shifting Your Mindset toward Opportunity.*** Enlisting the final principle helps shift our way of looking at conflict. Turning an internal abrasion into an opportunity makes it easier to see possibilities, and to see others as something other than simply villains. Developing the ability to make this shift requires practice. It takes persistent willingness to be introspective and to ask yourself questions like "What can I change?"

These five principles can be resources for confronting the habit of stepping away from relationships across difference when they become difficult. Any relationship becomes challenging in the midst of conflict and is often worth working on. But the relationships across difference are rare and precious resources that are both personally fulfilling and functionally essential if an organization is moving toward a Leveraging Difference capability.

### *Foster Organizational Understanding of Difference*

Understanding difference through individual and interpersonal learning is necessary, but it's not sufficient. Organizations that understand strategic differences gather information in more systematic ways as well. They conduct research with customers, employees, and other key stakeholders who can provide data and insight. They create processes to funnel information about relevant differences to the appropriate stakeholders.

Hyster Corp. is a manufacturer of lift trucks based in Greenville, North Carolina. The company's objective is to manufacture the safest, most effective equipment on the market. It has focused on the changing diversity mix of its customer organizations as a way of providing value-added service. Hyster collects data by having its engineers observe operators from customer organizations. They observe the use of older equipment before they develop new models, and new equipment after it is delivered to customers. In their observations, they make a point of factoring in the changing diversity of customer employees. They pay attention to the increasing average worker age, and to the relative physical capabilities of male and female operators. But Hyster also learned from observation and feedback that operator fatigue is a major issue, particularly in the last few hours of a work shift. Engineers saw operators move around on the platform, trying to get comfortable and avoid fatigue. Being aware of studies showing that the shoe sizes of workers are increasing, they increased the size of the platform on their new pallet trucks.[18] Such systems of end-user observation are a powerful way in which organizations gain intelligence about relevant differences. As was the case for Hyster, that observation can even lead to seeing new relevant differences.

Customer feedback systems aren't the only systemic sources for an understanding of relevant differences. Organizations use both internal resources and external partnerships to generate ongoing understanding and promote experimentation. American Express Company is a global services organization providing payment and travel-related products/services worldwide. It is the world's largest card issuer by purchase volume, processing millions of transactions daily for individual and commercial cardholders. The firm operates the world's largest travel network, serving both individual consumers and businesses.[19]

Like many other retail organizations, American Express has developed a market segmentation strategy that emphasizes understanding the communities and customers it serves worldwide. It tries to drive business growth by designing appropriate and appealing products and services for those constituents. To provide the necessary knowledge to expand into new markets, American Express developed a patent-pending process called Diverse Marketplace Intelligence (DMI). This system draws insights from both the firm's existing talent base and from strategically chosen external partners. The most prominent avenue for learning within the company is provided by employee network groups, such as those for Hispanic, black, and Muslim employees. External partners include nonprofit membership groups such as Catalyst, a research and advisory organization for advancing women in business, and the National Society for Hispanic MBAs.

An example of an innovation spawned by DMI is the Zync card, a charge card targeted toward young consumers. A key feature is that it lets consumers enroll in one of fourteen "Lifestyle Packs" that fall in the broad categories of travel, socializing, communicating, and eco/responsibility. Because there were fewer representatives of this younger demographic group internally at American Express, the firm needed to create an engaged community from which it could learn in order to develop this product. So it sponsored the 2010 One Young World inaugural symposium in London, sending five employee delegates and sponsoring five more nonemployee delegates. Through social networks including Facebook and Twitter, a Zync cardholder conversation was initiated in which cardholders could tell delegates which issues they wanted addressed and what questions they would like asked. This engaged community has subsequently been harnessed to influence how products are developed and how American Express markets to the demographic.

The effectiveness of DMI as a tool for understanding difference at American Express depends on its access to employees who carry knowledge about strategically relevant differences, and to the partnerships it can create to provide knowledge. Neither of these relies on specific individuals. Employees may come and go, and even partnerships may shift, but American Express has positioned itself to be able to test out new ideas for marketing to any demographic they pursue.

It is worth noting that the differences that are relevant for American Express are somewhat traditional. The previous example involved Millennials, people in the generation born in the last two decades of the twentieth century, but American Express also has had success with products for Hispanic and LGBT customers. Developing capabilities for Leveraging Difference does not mean *avoiding* traditional differences. It simply means not being constrained by them.

*The Importance of Acquiring a Missing Difference.* One vulnerability of the DMI process developed by American Express is that the company may find that it lacks internal resources for learning about a particular difference. Indeed, that is what happened with the Zync card: there were very few Millennials working at American Express. In that instance, the company created a "workaround" by engaging the community in a medium well suited for that demographic—social media. But in other instances, companies may find that they want internal resources for learning about a particular difference but haven't hired the people to provide them. In chapter 1, I highlighted some of the challenges in recruiting and hiring people who are likely to carry the requisite knowledge about a relevant difference.

But an added challenge is that the people who represent a relevant difference frequently are anathema to the culture of the organization. Consolidated Technologies,* a manufacturer of commercial heating systems, had established a distinctive capability for high quality in its production process. They had focused on achieving zero defects in one particular process and had built a reputation as the industry leader in executing that process. Becoming that good required recruiting and hiring meticulous, detail-oriented managers. But they also needed to innovate in both product and manufacturing process design. Consolidated was flush with managers trained to think in detail, but they were lacking in people who could think outside the box. Moreover, the company was hierarchically structured, and employees were conditioned to follow orders and procedures. To innovate, though, they needed people willing to take risks. The problem they faced was that the culture of order and risk aversion was so strong that innovators didn't want to join the company. Some were attracted by compensation, but they didn't last long.

To combat the challenge of a cultural mismatch, leaders must develop a strategically driven, single-minded focus on results. A number of leaders known for successfully increasing diversity in their organizations have approached talent acquisition in just this way. Henry Schacht was strongly committed to creating a diverse team of leaders as CEO at Cummins Engine Company and later Lucent Technologies.[20] Steve Reinemund talks about his passion for creating a similarly diverse team when he was CEO at PepsiCo. At one point he mandated that he would only approve new hires if they were women or persons of color. When his advisors cautioned him, he refused to back down.[21] Jamie Dimon, CEO of JPMorgan Chase, has been adamant about acquiring the needed difference:

> Look, it's all very wonderful, you've done great things, but you haven't moved the friggin' needle [on getting the right representation of talent]. And there is only one way to move the needle, and that is to be clear about results. I don't want to hear any more conversations at the leadership level about process and awareness-raising. I assume it's going to happen, and a lot of it's going to have to happen, but any conversation I have about the topic can only be about results.[22]

These leaders, though emphasizing traditional differences, were operating with clear and cogent strategic intent.

***Managing Resistance to Understanding Difference***

Understanding difference is inextricably linked to organizational change. As a result, it can foster anxiety and resistance among those who need to learn about relevant differences. One of the more prevalent activities designed to facilitate understanding difference in U.S. organizations has been diversity training, but even the best-designed training programs encounter pushback from participants.[23] This pushback occurs for different reasons. Learning about difference may signal that the status quo will shift, and that can be especially anxiety-provoking for those who hold positions of power and privilege in the current environment. They may resist because they don't want to lose that standing.[24]

Resistance can also result when activities promoting understanding difference include content that generates identity abrasions. Participants may be exposed to information about the business environment, society, and history that challenges their self-images in the context of the organization and even society as a whole. And finally resistance can emerge if an organization's practices and culture are in conflict with an openness to understanding difference. For some organizations, even a strategic imperative to understanding difference is hindered by longstanding cultural norms that reinforce their parochialism. Any or all of these factors can undermine an organization's attempt to promote understanding of relevant difference.

Elegance USA, Inc.,* a wholly owned subsidiary of the Elegance global cosmetics company, is located on the East Coast. It produces hair and skin products and fragrances for consumer and professional markets. Since its founding in 1953, the company's rapid growth has been fueled by the same traditions of excellence that characterize the parent company. Elegance USA has traditionally had a “boutique” culture about it. Despite its relationship to the parent company, its employees think of themselves as owning a special personal brand that sets them apart from any other operation in the world. Their high level of performance has contributed a kind of “diva” attitude as part of the organizational culture.

One of Elegance USA’s major challenges has been penetrating the markets for women of color. These markets were seen as today’s most significant growth opportunity, and the U.S. market presented a variety of opportunities. But the crossover was challenging because of the historical schism between women of color and white-dominated cosmetic companies like Elegance.[25] The cosmetics industry was trending toward positioning beauty products multiculturally, which had the benefit of being able to sell to women of all ethnicities. But Elegance realized they just didn’t know their customers well.

As part of their attempt to understand the differences in these markets, the Professional Products department planned presentations on African and African American, Arab, and South Asian cultures as a way of enhancing the company’s ability to market to these communities. The members of the working group were predominantly white and, by their own admission, had experienced limited contact with women from these groups. As they immersed themselves in learning, not all were enthusiastic. Several expressed reservations about investing time and resources when they could each learn enough just on their own initiative. After three learning sessions consisting of facilitated case discussion and role-playing, one of the women, Anne, became quite agitated. She said she resented being forced to attend these sessions like a “child in grade school.” In further conversation, she voiced what some other women were also feeling: she found it difficult to discuss issues of culture, race, and discrimination against people of color when she so acutely dealt with sexism on a daily basis. She found it exceedingly difficult to keep an open mind, especially when portions of what the group was learning focused on men from the different cultural groups.

Anne had a difficult time negotiating two facets of her identity. On the one hand, she strongly identified herself as a woman; that was her dominant view of her social group membership and shaped how she saw herself across a wide range of situations.[26] She was also white and American-born, but though she would not dispute either fact, she rarely thought of herself as just a white person or just an American. Training that focused on cultural and racial bias challenged Anne to put her primary group identity aside and consider parts of herself that she didn't typically see as central. This challenge was made all the more difficult because these were aspects of her identity that gave her societal privilege. Being white and being native-born are sources of higher status in the United States than being a person of color or being an immigrant. For people who identify primarily with a lower-status group (for example, females), it can be difficult to explore higher-status aspects of their identities.[27]

Leaders can help circumvent resistance in three ways. First, they need to be explicit and transparent about the strategic importance of understanding relevant differences in order to provide learners with a rationale for the activity. One of Anne's resistant behaviors was to insist that understanding could be achieved by individuals on their own time. This implied that understanding the relevant difference was not business critical, when of course it was. Learners are galvanized when a leader can provide a continuous and consistent credible message that the difference matters. The goal of the learning activity is to help members of the organization understand more deeply how to capitalize on that difference.

The second step that leaders can undertake is to create and support effective vehicles for understanding difference. This could range from ensuring that difference training is conducted by skilled facilitators to making sure that processes (like American Express's DMI) are well designed and implemented. The key task for the leader is to institute quality control and accountability for understanding-difference methodologies.

Finally, leaders must model understanding difference. They must participate in practices that promote understanding at every opportunity. This can take a variety of forms. A leader might serve as a resource for a project team that has a mandate to explore a relevant difference. Or a leader might enlist her assistants to join her in attending and then facilitating training modules to promote understanding of a relevant difference. At Landmark Communications, Inc., managers attended and then led workshops on how to leverage relevant differences in different parts of the business. A leader can also initiate and involve herself in relationships across differences, professionally and personally. By doing so, she sends the signal that behavior and practices that promote understanding difference are essential.

## How Understanding Encourages Seeing

In concluding this exploration of how leaders and organizations understand difference, one dilemma emerges: How can leaders see difference if they don't understand it? In the absence of some understanding of the difference, how can leaders effectively assess its relevance? From a practical perspective, of course, some potentially relevant differences will be missed if leaders simply have no point of reference for perceiving them. You have to understand at least a little bit about a difference for it to be seen as relevant.

But the more important dynamic on this part of the cycle is that seeing and understanding difference feed one another. It is possible to see a difference that is likely to be relevant, even without knowing much about it. Leaders may even use tacit understanding, experience, and intuition to decide whether a difference is relevant.[28] But once leaders establish a competency for understanding difference, they have two options with any difference they see.

First, they can move beyond perception or intuition to build verifiable knowledge that the difference is—or isn't—relevant. The tools outlined in this chapter will help them refine their understanding of the difference and, if it really is relevant, prepare to engage it. Or they can reject the difference as irrelevant and seek out other differences that are relevant.

Second, an enhanced understanding of a difference can reveal secondary differences. A team of human resource leaders, looking at the challenges of hiring Millennials, revamped their strategy once they realized that members of this generational group differed depending upon ethnic identity. They decided that they could segment their target market further and speak directly to Hispanic, Asian, and black Millennials in distinctive ways. Part of their original mistake, they concluded, was that they had been operating as though all Millennials had a common profile: the MTV Millennials. This exemplifies one way in which a new relevant difference can be seen as the result of understanding another difference.

Understanding difference is fundamentally a dynamic process. It is not simply gathering data and placing it in a file or on a bookshelf. It is a process of collecting and interacting with that information in ways that allow leaders and organizations to use it ultimately. Along the way, understanding is enhanced by taking risks, making mistakes, engaging in conflict—and learning from all of these. And this enhanced understanding sets the stage for engaging the difference.

## Key Takeaways

1. Understanding difference is the capacity to gather and integrate comprehensive and accurate knowledge about relevant differences.
2. In order to understand difference, leaders and managers must do these things:
   - Engage in individual learning: be curious and do research.
   - Learn in relationships: be inquisitive, listen, self-disclose, give and receive feedback, and manage conflict by pausing, connecting, questioning yourself, seeking balanced support, and shifting your mindset.
   - Develop organizational systems that help you understand difference.
   - Manage resistance to understanding by providing vision, managing the quality of learning vehicles, and modeling learning behavior.
3. Understanding difference can encourage seeing new relevant differences.

# 6

# Engaging Difference

*By Martin N. Davidson and Heather R. Wishik*

Engaging difference is the step in which organizations begin to change. Up to this point in the cycle, the focus has been on creating a foundation for intentional organizational action. In seeing difference, leaders worked to identify what differences might be relevant for generating organizational results. They started with strategy and used tools such as strategy maps to help hone in on differences that might be important to customers and markets, to strategic internal processes like manufacturing or supply chain development, and to workforce composition. They even looked at external stakeholders—government agencies, nonprofits, community organizations—that affected the ability of their organization to create value. In understanding difference, leaders guided their organizations through the process of learning about what these relevant differences mean to the stakeholders involved and how these relevant differences could impact organizational results. Labeling the difference as possibly relevant was just the first step. Developing a deeper working knowledge of the difference was the second step.

At the stage of engaging differences, organizations are moving to greater levels of coordinated action. Leaders begin to assess what difference reveals about current practices and to explore options for new approaches that could produce a desired business result related to the difference. Engaging difference requires commitment to the importance of the business opportunity offered by a given difference, and follow-through such as experimenting with new ways of doing things. It is these new approaches that allow the organization to begin to capitalize on difference. This step has a "trial and error" quality to it; some experiments work and some fail. But all of them yield insight about the relevant difference and how it might benefit the organization.

Organizations learn by acquiring knowledge, sharing it throughout the organization, and figuring out how to use it.[1] Leaders who create change through organizational learning about difference do so by promoting experimentation. Their work with seeing and understanding difference generates hypotheses about how difference could enhance the larger organization—some promising, some not. The task in engaging difference is to establish "laboratories" in which these hypotheses can be tested. This experimentation and the resources and risks it requires are a core part of engaging difference. The following experiments conducted in a variety of companies illustrate the scope of possible investigations and the learning that can result.

Engaging difference is also the point at which leaders truly have "skin in the game." Seeing and understanding difference are fundamentally preparatory activities, but engaging difference is where a leader's commitment becomes visible. This is a crossroads that is often the place of greatest resistance. Leaders must be skillful in generating buy-in from at least a few internal stakeholders

**Figure 5 Engaging Difference**

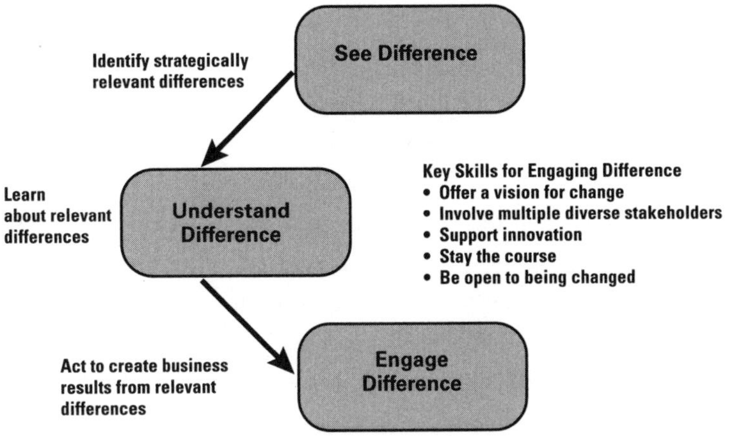


who can help enact a change that may not yet seem important to others. The tide of energy and enthusiasm that flows from active experimentation can foster commitment from additional key players.

## How to Engage Difference

The story of MedTown Pharmaceuticals* and its path toward engaging difference helps illuminate several of the steps a leader must follow to move from *seeing* difference to *engaging* difference. MedTown is a national corporation that operates retail pharmacy outlets as well as nursing home and mail-in pharmacy services. It has a supply chain that includes distribution centers. As it grew from regional scale to national through acquisitions and expansion, it needed to add distribution centers. Supply chain leader Mark Manning* considered the opportunity to start one or more distribution centers from scratch.

### *Seeing Difference at MedTown*

Manning had been a leader at other companies where issues of difference were discussed. Now he asked himself what differences might make a difference in designing new facilities. After some reflection he came up with four things he wanted his team to consider as they planned the new centers:

- Manning noted the very tight profit margin with which MedTown operates—often only a few pennies per item sold—and the need to squeeze efficiencies out of every process. This meant factoring in the distance from long-haul truck routes and rail depots, for example. And he wanted to be sure that in choices about site selection as well as building and process design, the company would find innovative ways to make the new building more efficient.
- He pointed out issues related to the aging workforce in the United States and the fact that work at distribution centers tends to be quite physical.
- He noted the regional shortages of a labor force willing to take hourly work for pay only slightly above minimum wage.
- He highlighted the fact that people with disabilities are chronically underemployed or unemployed, making them potentially available as a workforce.

Manning asked his team to plan an efficient distribution center that could set a goal of having a reliable workforce, of which 40 percent would be people with disabilities—full-time, regularly employed workers meeting the same quality and output requirements as anyone else.

### *Understanding Difference at MedTown*

Manning's team gasped at what felt like a Big Hairy Audacious Goal (BHAG), and then they set to work.[2] Some team members reviewed the processes in the existing distribution centers, looking for processing stages that were bottlenecks or took significant worker time. They searched for building, technology, and process redesigns that could increase efficiency and be cost effective. Another part of the team reached out to service and training organizations for the disabled to learn more about job training programs and types of disabilities that might fit the distribution center job requirements.

A third group worked with the American Association of Retired Persons (AARP) and other experts on aging to figure out what accommodations were available for carrying out physical tasks such as lifting and moving heavy objects. Meanwhile, the real estate group examined census and other data to find sites that had four characteristics: long-haul trucking and rail routes were easily accessible; the available hourly workforce was stable or growing; public transportation was available; and disability services were strong.

### *Engaging Difference at MedTown*

The three subgroups and real estate met together to show each other what they had learned before reporting back to Manning. They put a map of the country up on the wall. The real estate people went first, starring the locations that met all four goals. There were only three in the U.S. The disability group went next. They explained they had learned that many individuals with developmental disabilities such as autism spectrum disorders or Down syndrome could probably be trained to do the distribution center work, particularly if the training and computer-based processing tasks involved pictures and symbols and not too much print. At this point the process improvement subgroup interrupted to report that they had found that some steps that currently required a lot of keystrokes could be speeded up if the distribution center shifted to touchscreens with symbols and pictures.

Someone from the aging-workforce group jumped in to say that there was a best-practice standard for computer work for aging workers suggesting that touchscreens cause fewer repetitive motion injuries than keyboards, and that symbols are easier than print for aging eyes to see. They also noted that adjustable height for all desktop or tabletop tasks, such as product processing, was another best practice. The disability group shouted "Ditto" on that one, and the process improvement group shouted "Ditto" again! They had learned that working at an inappropriate height slows down workers and increases risk of injury. There was a moment of silence as group members looked at one another. Finally one of them said, "You know, we might really be able to do this!"

The group members recommended to Manning that a purpose-built distribution center should be proposed to the three localities that real estate had identified. The building and process design would include touchscreen computer processes using symbols; automated box-lifting and moving equipment to permit unloading and loading by individual operators; wheelchair-accessible aisles and entries; adjustable-height processing stations; building entries accessible for buses and vans; and preferred parking for van pools.

The three localities, and their local disability services, would be asked to develop proposals for operating (with government funding) an onsite training facility that MedTown would build and equip. Disability services would use the center to train people for full-time employment in the building, and older workers could learn how to operate the lifting equipment and the touch screens. The training program would be designed collaboratively by MedTown and disability services. The locality would have to agree to route public transport in and out of the building's entry drive if it didn't already stop very close by.

Manning was amazed by the report and endorsed it after reading the projected cost figures. He got approval from the rest of MedTown's leadership, with slight modification to first retrofit and expand an existing distribution center and then invite two localities to bid for construction on one new facility.

In the MedTown story, a number of critical steps are evident. First, engaging difference often requires a leader to *offer a vision of business benefits to be seized* and communicate strong belief in that vision. Then, because engaging difference is grounded in coordinated action, it usually needs to *involve multiple stakeholders* and work units. And engaging difference calls for a leader to *support innovative activity*—incorporating new information and looking at what's already known in new ways to enhance processes and products. It involves willingness to take risk; people may feel uncomfortable with the change in general and with the differences connected to the change, like disability. But leaders must *stay the course*. Even well-planned attempts to engage difference sometimes yield fuzzy results for a while until the impact of the difference can actually be measured. Finally, engaging difference often means a leader must *be open to being changed.*

## Offer a Vision of Benefits to Be Seized

As with any organizational change initiative, leadership must provide a compelling vision of the need for change as well as a vision of the path forward.[3] It is extremely difficult to mobilize action in the absence of a model for the future. In the Leveraging Difference Cycle, a need for change can be obscured by two factors. People naturally resist change in the absence of good reason for changing; leaders must provide that compelling reason. Also, for reasons discussed in previous chapters, people often find reasons to discount the importance of difference-related change. It could be because of bias, or because they don't feel competent to engage the relevant difference. Leaders seeking to engage difference may be faced with resistance, apathy, or both.

This makes it all the more important for a leader to be clear and confident about the need to engage difference. The real business benefits to be gleaned from a difference may, at first, be evident only to the leader. Therefore he or she needs to convey that conviction to key stakeholders until they, too, share it. Mark Manning believed there was an opportunity to gain efficiencies and to replenish his labor force. He also realized the urgency of doing so, thanks to MedTown's low-margin business model and its aging workforce. He communicated to his team the issues and his strong belief in the need for change.

Sometimes this clarity motivates followers because they respect the leader and take up the charge on his or her word. But sometimes skepticism about the leader's analysis challenges followers to prove him or her wrong. This was what happened in Manning's case. His people didn't share his belief at first, but his conviction helped move them to learn. Either way, the leader must use clarity of vision to motivate people to act.

### Involve Multiple Stakeholders

To be effective, engaging difference activity typically involves a multiple and diverse array of stakeholders. Two factors contribute to the need for this array of contributors to the engaging difference effort. First, substantive change cannot take hold without the buy-in of key stakeholders who can then sell it to their constituents.[4] And because engaging difference activity is experimental, and designed to lead to larger change, it is best to include multiple stakeholders in the early stages. It could be much more difficult to garner their support once the blueprint for change has been set, when they are likely to feel ignored and disrespected and thus more inclined to resist the change. Moreover, since working with relevant difference is the essence of the activity, it is often useful to enlist participants who embody some of those differences.

Another factor that necessitates involving diverse stakeholders is that this activity requires information about differences that is likely to be both novel and complex. The information will be novel because the mandate of the engaging difference team is to explore innovation. If they are not bringing together new information or combining old information in new ways, they are probably not doing their job. The information may be complex because the team is being challenged to think about routine work in a much more nuanced way.

When the subgroups at MedTown pooled their findings, the power of multiple stakeholders working together was evident. They brought together a great deal of information—insights about autism and Down syndrome, training techniques and learning styles, equipment design (use of pictures and symbols), and human factors engineering (use of touchscreens, adjusting table heights). This was a lot for them to process, and having multiple contributors was essential to the project. Teams with multiple diverse stakeholders manage information better, innovate more, and provide superior results.

## Support Innovative Approaches

Engaging difference is an innovative activity. Its purpose is to transform established processes by introducing elements of relevant difference. Ultimately it is a creative activity. That was apparent at MedTown, and it was also evident at Patriot Health Care.* Patriot is a not-for-profit health maintenance organization (HMO) and health insurer. Its medical director recognized that changes in demographics in its primary operating region, New England, were impacting the quality of health care outcomes. In emergency rooms, patients who spoke little or no English were not getting appropriate care, or not getting it quickly enough, because of the language barrier. In outpatient and nonemergency treatment, cultural barriers were interfering with provider–patient communication and patient compliance with medical advice.

These problems resulted in higher medical costs and lower service quality. Doctors, physician assistants, and nurses were feeling frustrated at the lapses in patient compliance and ongoing communication failures. The situation was increasing the risk of malpractice issues. Patriot faced a problem: raise insurance rates and risk more frequent malpractice claims, or solve the cross-cultural challenges.

Understanding what was happening allowed Patriot to put most of its focus on the languages needed in the emergency rooms—Spanish and Portuguese—and focus less on other languages, like Vietnamese, Cambodian, Laotian, and Russian. Patriot contracted with a medical anthropologist to help it learn about the major differences between U.S.-based medical practices and the beliefs and practices of various groups of patients. For example, there was an influx of Southeast Asians, including Vietnamese, Cambodians, Laotians, and Hmong. Herbal remedies and shamanic interventions aimed at appeasing spirits or correcting perceived imbalances were among the traditional practices related to illness that the anthropologist described.

Patriot recognized that as an HMO and medical insurance provider for these populations, it might be cost effective to develop certified medical translators as well as cross-cultural training programs for its medical care providers. They researched the matter and concluded that training for both purposes was a product unavailable in New England. To create and manage such programs, to be offered to health care providers inside and outside Patriot's networks, Patriot decided to create a foundation. Since 1980 this foundation has offered medical interpreter classes and certification programs as well as cultural insight classes for health care providers. Providers are taught about various cultural explanations of illness and healing so that they can collaborate with shamans and other healers. They also provide treatment advice in terms that can co-exist with cultural beliefs.

The engaging difference process was highly innovative at Patriot, as it was at MedTown. At Patriot, the creation of the foundation and training programs—themselves innovative—led to other structural changes and opportunities. Once the foundation existed, Patriot was able to use it for additional purposes, including the coordination of employee volunteerism and to support a project for community access to health care. At MedTown, the process redesign involved several significant innovations: touchscreens, automated box-lifting, and even establishing the training center to work with people with disabilities to prepare them to be new full-time employees.

The competencies a leader must develop to support the innovation that engaging difference fosters depend, in part, on the kinds of projects undertaken. Manning's MedTown initiative focused on innovation in process redesign. Other initiatives might focus on product innovation or on complex innovation requiring expertise in different areas.[5] However, broad leadership themes emerge as being important for fostering innovative work: empowering others to do their work; enabling collaboration among team members; encouraging contributions from diverse perspectives; accepting the inevitability of mistakes and failures; and providing organizational and political support for the creative work.[6] Interestingly, it is also important for leaders to be able to resist becoming individual contributors and getting into the weeds of the work. Leaders are most effective at driving innovation when they are providing the best conditions for their people to be creative.

Another trait a leader needs to support innovation is the courage to take risks. Engaging difference means leading an organization into uncharted territory. Organizational culture that emphasizes risk aversion can make the journey even more perilous. But engaging difference will always feel risky, and the ideas it generates will seem edgy. This was true for Ray Davis, the president of Umpqua Bank. Umpqua had catered to the loggers and farmers in rural Oregon since its 1953 founding as South Umpqua State Bank, and the bank was known for its welcoming, unpretentious customer service.[7] Over the years Umpqua had expanded, and by 2002 it included almost seventy branches in a network that spanned the state. But that expansion had come at a relatively steep price. Following a frenzied period of mergers and acquisitions, the organization had not been able to transmit its friendly, community-oriented culture throughout its network. Customers who were used to dealing with other banks had no idea what to expect from the new Umpqua Bank.

Davis worried that in the competitive world of banking, these early signs of brand dilution signaled a potential loss of brand identity and customer focus. Putting his stake in the ground on the belief that the physical bank environment was a crucial component of Umpqua's identity, Davis focused on creating the "next generation" Umpqua Bank, beginning with the design of a new branch in Portland. Instead of hiring an architectural firm that specializes in working for banks to design an appealing but conventional interior environment, Davis hired ZIBA, an industrial design firm that ordinarily designed objects, and had absolutely no experience in the banking industry. The ZIBA team members knew how to design, but they had absolutely no experience with banks; they brought a truly different perspective.

The role Davis wanted this firm to play was that of key collaborator in the new bank design. Working with the Umpqua team, ZIBA's job would first be to act as a catalyst for defining the essence of the bank's brand. Then, working with the architectural firm TVA, its next task would be to generate insights and ideas about how to create a new physical environment consistent with that brand.

ZIBA's collaboration with the Umpqua management team crystallized the bank's understanding of its brand and customers. Then the collaboration with TVA resulted in the creation of a unique banking environment. The Umpqua branch is more reminiscent of a hotel lobby or an upscale retail establishment than a typical bank. Coffee, newspapers, and comfortable chairs arranged in a cafe-style sitting area encourage people to relax and stay a while. To enhance socializing, Umpqua sponsors community events such as book readings and knitting clubs. What customers experience when they step into this branch is a sense of comfortable, unpretentious, community-oriented credibility—exactly the brand positioning that Davis wanted to strengthen. As a measure of the effectiveness of that effort, nine months after opening the Portland branch Umpqua Bank had exceeded its initial goal of $15 million in new deposits by $20 million, racking up more than $35 million in deposits for the period.

Davis was clear on the strategic goal he wanted to pursue. But the relevant difference he identified as essential was "Umpqua-ness." He needed to marshal the perspective of outsiders to generate the change he thought was needed. He enlisted ZIBA because they were highly qualified, and what looked like a liability—that they didn't know the bank or the industry—was, for Davis, an asset. ZIBA team members wouldn't be encumbered by pressure to do things "the Umpqua way" or "the banking way." He relied on collaboration with ZIBA to provide the bank's internal leaders with a clear understanding about Umpqua/non-Umpqua differences. And then he turned the firm loose to create a truly innovative design. Davis took a risk. But he used difference to create something that would serve an important strategic purpose. That is the essence of engaging difference.

## Stay the Course

Whether with patience, resolve, or both, leaders engaging difference must persist in their commitment and support of engaging difference efforts, even when they are pressured to back off. It may take time for clarity about a specific experiment to emerge. For space reasons, MedTown's retrofitted distribution center had placed its training center in a separate building. As a result, the company struggled to figure out how to make the training seem real enough to prepare people with disabilities for functioning in the actual distribution setting. The physical distance between structures impeded that ability of participants to actually apply what they learned to the distribution work. And the physical arrangement made the training center seem like a nice accommodation but not a serious effort to change the distribution process. Modifying the experience so that trainees spent more time at the actual worksite helped; it just took some time to fine-tune the process until it was working as intended.

## Be Open to Being Changed

Leading an engaging difference effort can feel like being swept up by a current at times. One of the challenges for a leader is to let go of the need to exert control over the process. It is critical to offer guidance, direction, and oversight, but the leader cannot prescribe or micromanage the activity. It just isn't possible. To engage difference is to introduce potentially overwhelming amounts of new information and to use it to overhaul familiar processes and practices. We have discussed at length how that can challenge employees. But it can also challenge the leader, even if he or she is the one who started the ball rolling.

The leader is also human, and even though he or she may be psychologically more prepared for change than others in the organization, that doesn't mean that it won't be jarring when it arrives. At MedTown, Manning was delighted at the work his subgroups had accomplished, but he was also quite surprised to hear their recommendations. For many leaders, the line between wonder and apprehension may be a thin one.

Change related to engaging difference can add an element of surprise for a leader. Engaging difference activity involves collecting information, and there are times when that information may be surprising, challenging, or upsetting. Whether it's statistics on the incidence of disability or stories from people who have been marginalized in an organization, the leader's view of her organization, herself, or the larger world may be challenged. The best a leader can do is to remain open and curious. Assume that there will be surprising or challenging results, and they may be easier to digest when they come your way.

### Caveat: Not All Experiments Are Successful

Engaging difference can be extremely difficult. The examples cited thus far capture the exciting possibilities of what can be created. Of course, not all experimentation yields such positive outcomes. But even when an experiment doesn't end up achieving a specific goal—such as increased sales or lower costs—there usually has been learning that will help the organization be ready for the next difference-related opportunity.

As an example, a national hardware chain's experiment with increasing its inventory of outdoor cooking equipment and accessories for stores with large Hispanic customer bases didn't at first result in the sales they had expected. They had studied various differences relevant to their Hispanic customers and thought they understood that grilling was something this population often did. After examining what had happened, merchandising leaders realized that their Hispanic base included a substantial number of stores in areas like Miami and Chicago, where many customers were apartment or condo dwellers who didn't have access to outdoor grilling spaces. When they changed the list of locations to which they allocated outdoor cooking equipment to focus on places where more Hispanic customers live in houses—like Atlanta, South Carolina, and Texas—they did see incremental sales increases. Engagement experiments sometimes push an organization back to the drawing board to do more work on understanding a difference. Then the experiment must be adjusted before positive outcomes can be seen.

## Almost There

Engaging difference—the final step on the path to Leveraging Difference—is the component that involves an organization's systems and culture most directly. The best engagement experiments begin on a relatively small scale and are carefully measured and communicated. When leaders ignore these two things, the experiments are less likely to produce the desired results. But whether an experiment is successful or not, the lessons it teaches can fuel more engagement and strengthen the organization's capability to leverage difference.

Many leaders make the mistake of assuming that engaging difference is the desired endpoint for effectively leveraging difference. But when companies are merely engaging difference, they are still involved in tactical activity. They are feeling their way forward, trying out programs, policies, or training curricula that may or may not lead to incremental change. Leveraging difference, on the other hand, is the manifestation of a new capability that integrates difference-related activities with the organization's core capabilities.

## Key Takeaways

1. Engaging difference is the stage of the Leveraging Difference Cycle at which leaders and organizations are moving to greater levels of coordinated action.

2. To engage difference, leaders must cultivate five competencies:
   - Offer a vision of the business benefits of engaging the relevant difference.
   - Involve multiple diverse stakeholders in the activity.
   - Support innovation.
   - Stay the course.
   - Be open to being changed.

# 7

# Becoming a Leveraging Difference Organization

*By Martin N. Davidson & Heather R. Wishik*

> Multinational manufacturer Procter & Gamble's business is innovation.... To build and foster a culture of innovation, P&G has entrenched diversity as a key principle in the workplace and leveraged the skilled immigrant talent pool.... In addition to creating a diverse employee mix internally, P&G is open to and prides itself on collaboration with external partners....
>
> P&G can now identify promising ideas throughout the world and apply its own research and development, manufacturing, marketing, and purchasing capabilities to create better and cheaper products faster.... P&G's leaders turned difference into advantage....[1]

How does an organization become like this? How does it come to leverage difference?

Ultimately, organizations that are leveraging difference begin to generate results in increasingly effortless ways. It's like that moment when you've been riding your bicycle with training wheels and suddenly you can balance without them, and pick up speed. The entire organization begins to think in terms of how differences are relevant and how they contribute to results. This becomes standard operating procedure. Learning about the implications of difference becomes a way of life for everyone in the organization. As Mark Settles of JPMorgan Chase phrased it, people are living Leveraging Difference.

How do organizations make that shift from engaging difference to leveraging it?

## How You Know When You're Leveraging Difference

Organizations develop a capability for Leveraging Difference through hard work, discipline, and imagination. When they are consistently leveraging differences, a quantum shift seems to occur. Leaders make sure they are seeing the differences that matter. They pay meticulous attention to strategy and identify the differences that could help them execute on that strategy. They are mindful about not letting biases and conventional ways of thinking cause them to miss important differences. They set in motion activity to help determine how those differences affect results for the organization. Stakeholders do their homework. They begin to reach out to colleagues and establish cross-difference relationships that will further their understanding. They develop systems within the organization and partnerships with outside organizations that can be resources for information about differences.

Then leaders begin to turn that knowledge into action. They engage difference by establishing projects that serve as experiments in using the relevant difference to generate positive results. They make sure these experiments involve multiple diverse stakeholders, and they take special care to create space for participants to be innovative. Leaders are firm in their resolve to let a project run its course, resisting any pressure to stop and return to doing business as usual.

Moving from being an organization that conducts a successful engaging difference experiment here and there to an organization that embraces a Leveraging Difference capability takes significant time and effort. Organizations that have done so are distinguished by two characteristics. First, they are achieving short-term results; they are able to see that the engaging difference experiments are working. Second, they "recycle" the Leveraging Difference Cycle. They apply it to multiple differences to address a variety of strategic challenges.

### *Solving Problems with Engaging Difference Experiments*

All engaging difference experiments, successful or not, yield lessons that can help organizations improve. But from a practical standpoint, the successful ones make the biggest impact. Part of the transition from engaging difference to fully leveraging difference happens because stakeholders inside and outside the organization experience difference-related success. One measure of success is the bottom-line result: if the experiment helped meet a business objective, that success matters immensely. But a second dimension of success is the process by which the difference was engaged. The extent to which the Leveraging Difference capability spreads throughout the organization depends on both these success factors.

*Success by Achieving Measurable Goals.* When Patriot Health Care started its foundation to create and manage medical translation and cross-cultural competency programs, that structure was instrumental in delivering the interpreter classes and cultural insight classes that helped health care providers offer help in culturally appropriate ways. The goal was to become more cost-effective without sacrificing quality of care. It worked: costs of care related to culture and language differences decreased, medical outcomes improved, and jobs as interpreters were created for people with linguistic skills. A similar success occurred as a result of how Med-Town Pharmaceuticals engaged difference in its facility project. One facility was retrofitted and another was built at the locality with the winning bid. Both have achieved the desired efficiencies. Moreover, the retrofitted facility is closing in on the goal of 40 percent workers with disabilities.

These kinds of successes are clear, visible, and compelling. A goal is set and either achieved or exceeded, or the trend toward success is so strong that observers are confident the goal will be reached. Tangible results energize those who advocated using relevant differences to create results. More importantly, they capture the attention of those who have been oblivious to the possibilities. Those who are simply resistant to the highlighting of difference may not be enamored with the process, but they will pay attention to bottom-line results.

One other point about achieving these results is worth mentioning: Often they are low-hanging fruit. Often when engaging difference endeavors have been completed and are successful, those involved wonder at the relative simplicity of the actual experiment. It's not that seeing and understanding the critical differences was a trivial process—those activities often take time and effort. But once people roll up their sleeves and get to work, they are often pleasantly surprised by how dramatic the result is, given the relatively modest amount of effort it takes.

Hewitt Associates is a global provider of HR services, and one of its core consulting areas is retirement management.[2] With their clients' staffs becoming more diverse, Hewitt realized it needed to consider new strategies. For example, one U.S. client found that its employees were tapping into retirement savings plans in very different ways. It was also clear that the differences followed ethnic cultural lines. The main demographic groups—the differences Hewitt saw—were Hispanics, whites, Asians, and blacks. A culturally diverse team was assigned the task of better understanding these differences as they related to retirement savings management.

The team investigated how people from the different cultural groups perceived money and saved for the future. Building on research they had previously done on 401(k) behavior, Hewitt looked more closely at ethnicity relative to retirement savings.[3] The team hypothesized that perceptions of money that were so different would affect retirement contributions. When they tested this hypothesis by conducting a large survey, they learned that even after controlling for factors such as age, salary, and job tenure, black and Hispanic workers had lower participation rates and contributed less to their 401(k) plans than their white and Asian counterparts. Blacks and Hispanics were also more likely to have taken a loan and/or a hardship withdrawal from their 401(k) accounts, significantly compromising their chances for a comfortable retirement.

With this knowledge in hand, Hewitt tailored communications about planning more effectively to different communities, and this resulted in increased contributions from blacks and Hispanics. Changing the savings patterns of clients in these groups only required understanding the group dynamics and making straightforward changes to processes and products. It was low-hanging fruit—Hewitt just needed to learn how to pick it.

Interestingly, the success of an engaging difference experiment is sometimes enhanced by repeating the project in other contexts within the organization. An innovative discovery made in one part of a business may not be wholeheartedly adopted in a different part—the context might be different enough that the idea doesn't seem to make sense. Nonetheless, it can be useful to replicate engaging difference experiments in other parts of the organization where benefits could be achieved. Even if the experiment fails in the second context, the organization continues to become more intelligent about the conditions under which it can leverage a given difference. Hewitt's discovery of the variations in savings behavior among U.S. clients spurred them to look more granularly at populations in Canada. They began conducting similar explorations there using a different profile of ethnicity there, with the next steps remaining to be determined.[4]

***Success by Generating Energy.*** While achieving tangible goals is critical in establishing the Leveraging Difference capability, even more important might be the enthusiasm created in the process. Engaging difference activity frequently stimulates excitement, creativity, and energy—not surprising, since the leadership tone in a Leveraging Difference approach is one of new possibilities. Positive energy is contagious and can inspire the whole team to work together more effectively.[5] Recall the interactions of the MedTown subgroups. As team members shared what they were learning, the light bulbs began to turn on. They worked in a collaborative space, with a map on the wall. As subgroups presented information, connections began to emerge. The disability and aging-worker groups found related information about user interfaces that led to the recommendation of touch screens. Individuals were increasingly energized not only by what they had learned in their own research, but also by what they were creating together.

What is also intriguing about this phenomenon of increased energy among teams is that collective enthusiasm can serve to give voice to team members who might feel silenced or marginalized elsewhere in the organization. In the classic 1957 film *Twelve Angry Men,* a jury must deliberate on the case of a teenage boy accused of murdering his father. As the film unfolds the jury debates and discusses and, in dramatic form, comes to a surprising decision. One of the most interesting elements of the film is how the jurors engage with one another. One character is particularly noteworthy in the context of a discussion about how difference, when engaged, creates energy. Early in the film, this character—a man from the slums—is reticent, refusing to express his opinion even when asked. When another juror inadvertently makes an insulting comment about people from the slums, he reacts with anger and resentment. But as the film proceeds the man changes. By the time the jury is nearing its decision, he is not only engaged and expressive, he helps other jurors understand a fact in the case by drawing on his own life experience. Over the course of the film he moves from being ashamed to speak to enthusiastically volunteering intelligence gathered from his poverty-stricken upbringing. Dramatic it may be, but it illustrates the contagious effect of energy on a work group.

Needless to say, a dysfunctional group process also has the potential to destroy rather than create energy. It could disenfranchise marginal members instead of empowering them. Whether teams working on an engaging difference experiment are effective or dysfunctional depends on how well they are designed and managed. But if they *are* effective, the energy they generate could be a critical tool in promoting the Leveraging Difference capability beyond the team. Team members may become advocates, communicating the benefits of the Leveraging Difference experiment to colleagues who had been uninformed or uninterested previously. Being able to show tangible results, of course, makes that communication all the more compelling.

### *Reiterating the Leveraging Difference Cycle*

Organizations that have fully developed a Leveraging Difference capability continue to follow the steps in the cycle for any emerging differences they see as relevant. An inevitability of organizational life—and life in our global society—is that differences will always be with us. There will always be new opportunities to leverage difference. In the United States, race and gender may have dominated the conversation about difference in the latter half of the twentieth century, but it's not as though there all sorts of other differences were not present. Organizations had stakeholders—employees, customers, partners—of different ethnicities, nationalities, sexual orientations, physical abilities, styles of thought, and more. This will continue to be true. New differences will become visible in organizations all over the world as we learn more about the diversity in our global society, and as we manage the biases and distortions that keep us from seeing differences that matter.

Leaders who want to make the most of these differences must continue to use the Leveraging Difference Cycle as a tool. By applying the cycle to emerging differences consistently, leaders accomplish a couple of things. They tackle pressing business challenges with the possibility of solving them in innovative ways. More importantly, they drive the Leveraging Difference capability more deeply into the fabric of their organizations. Eventually the activity becomes well learned and routine, and in this way the capability sustains itself.

For the Progressive School, introduced in Chapter 2, one of the challenges was the disparity in students' ratings of teaching quality for men and women on the faculty. Men's ratings were consistently higher, even though there was generally no difference in teaching assignments, class size, or other obvious structural factors. The phenomenon affected performance evaluations, promotion rates, and talent retention, and the school leadership worried that a buzz was developing in the recruiting market that Progressive was tough on women.

A committee appointed to address the issue used the Leveraging Difference Cycle. They identified gender as the relevant difference and conducted an employee climate survey to better understand the experiences of men and women faculty at the school. They observed and interviewed several male and female faculty members. These were challenging interviews, since many people were afraid to speak openly about gender disparities at the school. The committee's findings led them to hypothesize that part of the problem might be the classrooms themselves. The school's primary method of teaching was case studies, traditionally taught in amphitheater-style classrooms—large, semicircular rooms with three to five tiers rising toward the back of the room. The instructor stood front and center in the "pit." This setup appeared to benefit taller people, who could be seen more easily from all the tiers. It also seemed to benefit people with louder voices. And taller people with louder voices most often were men, not women.

The school implemented a simple experiment based on what the committee had learned. Lavaliere microphones would now be available as standard equipment in all classrooms so that any faculty member could use them. Within one school year, the disparity in ratings had been reduced by almost 10 percent. Most faculty members actually chose to use the microphones, men as well as women. Of course, the school only had one year of data to go on, and the remaining disparity remained troubling. The committee's work was not done; more experiments were in order. But committee members and the dean were encouraged by their method—so much so that when conflicts began to emerge between salaried and hourly staff, the dean decided to use the cycle again. Working with the salaried/hourly difference as the relevant one, a task force began with a schoolwide climate survey. They are now conducting interviews and collecting benchmarking data from competitor schools. Progressive School has not yet completed this iteration of the cycle, but they are encouraged that the process can help—a natural response to a successful tool. Whether or not the school's leadership continues to use of cycle will determine the extent to which Progressive becomes a Leveraging Difference institution.

When the Leveraging Difference capability is fully at work, the entire organization is routinely moving through the cycle, not just one or two departments. As experiments flourish, best practice is shared across departments and silos and the seeds of organizational learning are bearing fruit. It is important that the cycle of taking these steps becomes integrated into the way planning, strategy development, and decision-making are conducted. Positive results breed energy and commitment.

*Feedback Loops within the Cycle.* For simplicity's sake, I have presented the Leveraging Difference Cycle as a sequence of steps, and the implication has been that the cycle always follows this sequence. The diagram I presented in Chapter 3 (page 76) was quite linear: see a difference, understand it, and then engage it. In reality, it may not work exactly this way. These different steps may happen simultaneously, and with multiple differences. A glimpse of this was evident in the MedTown example, where several differences were explored in concert. And understanding one difference may lead to seeing another difference that was previously invisible. The more a marketing manager learns about Hispanic women customers, the more she begins to see Cuban, Puerto Rican, Mexican, and Dominican cultures as specific markets. Whereas all had been lumped under the label "Hispanic" before, with her enhanced lens she was motivated to better understand each culture.

Engaging difference provides many opportunities for stakeholders to deepen their understanding. Fundraisers at a prominent global nonprofit organization realized they needed to attract gay and lesbian donors, a pool with which they had had little success. The exclusively heterosexual and U.S.-born team of fundraisers experimented by talking frankly and openly to their few existing gay and lesbian donors about how to reach out to potential donors. The dialogue helped them gain access to venues where they could meet high-income gays and lesbians, and their experiences at those venues deepened the team's understanding about sexual orientation, both in the United States and elsewhere. They learned about sexual orientation as well as cultural norms in China, Vietnam, and Singapore. Even difference that is fully leveraged frequently leads to more seeing, understanding, and engaging. These feedback loops are captured in Figure 6.

All of this suggests an even richer understanding of how the Leveraging Difference capability could manifest itself. Not only may there be feedback loops in play as a team works on a particular difference-related challenge. But additional teams may be working

**Figure 6 Feedback Loops in the Leveraging Difference Cycle**

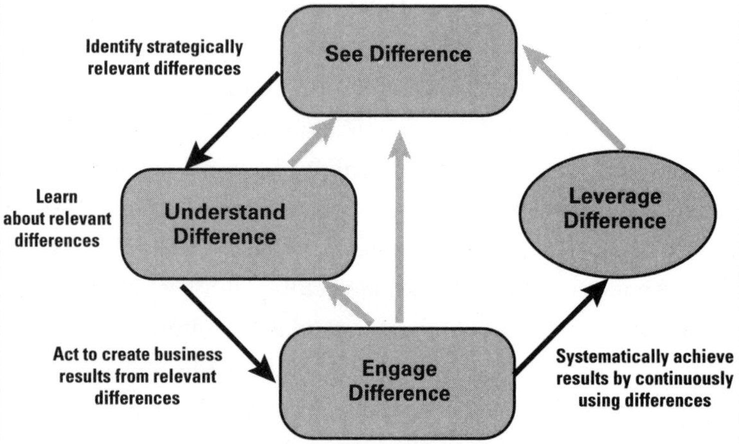


with other differences at the same time. Given effective channels of communication and collaboration, any number of cycles might be "fed" by other cycles within an organization. For an organization fueled by the vision of transforming difference into competitive advantage, it's an intriguing prospect.

## How Leaders Move their Organizations to Leveraging Difference

With this glimpse of what the Leveraging Difference capability looks like and how it can transform an organization, what can leaders do to foster this capability?

### *Work the Cycle Relentlessly*

Leaders build a Leveraging Difference capability by working though the Leveraging Difference Cycle relentlessly. Using the skills outlined throughout this book, a leader can regularly work on the various components—seeing, understanding, engaging—of the Leveraging Difference capability.

But leaders must influence and enlist others to work through the cycle, too. The more people who become comfortable with this tool, the easier it will be to see opportunities to use it (and to recognize when it's *not* likely to be helpful). The word "influence" is significant. Leaders who advocate for using the cycle won't necessarily have positional power over those they want to use it. Often these advocates will be leading from the middle of the organization. Nevertheless, the objective is the same wherever a leader is situated: get others to work the cycle, too.

#### *Communicate, Communicate, Communicate*

Successes that flow from the effective engagement of difference are isolated anomalies if there's no communication about them. One of the core tenets of any organizational change is the importance of communication about the change to a variety of stakeholders. Difference-related change is no different.

But it's also a reality that communicating about difference will be viewed as a risky proposition. This issue surfaced in chapter 5 in exploring the risks leaders sometimes feel when communicating about difference at an interpersonal level. In communicating about Leveraging Difference, leaders are also vulnerable to the risks involved in any public communication about difference. Will the message be skillfully delivered? Is the message clear and unambiguous? Will certain constituents be offended? Is there anything in the communication that places the organization at risk with external stakeholders (such as government entities, partner organizations, local communities)?

Fortunately, leaders have some assets they can call upon to help mitigate the risks. One of these is strategic clarity about why relevant differences matter to the organization. This helps them to communicate a powerful story that can be embraced by the organization's leaders. Frankly, one of the challenges many leaders have in communicating about diversity is that while they may have passion, they often don't have strategic clarity. Consistent with the discussion of the difficulty that a Managing Diversity frame can present when it comes to legitimate pushback, leaders sometimes feel they are not on secure footing in talking about diversity because they don't know how to think about this pushback. Indeed, sometimes their own commitment is compromised because they themselves have reservations about the importance of difference. Having a Leveraging Difference frame and the accompanying skills that comprise that capability can greatly diminish the apprehension leaders may harbor in talking about difference.

Another asset leaders can take advantage of is access to counselors: they can enlist help. Experts in communications, law, marketing, human resources, operations, or any other area can help them with the mechanics of their communications.

### *Encourage People Involved in the Cycle*

Leaders promote the Leveraging Difference capability by encouraging and supporting those who are involved in the cycle. An engaging difference project is likely to pool people who don't usually work together to consider issues that involve some tension or urgency. They are likely to be putting in extra time in order to accomplish their normal tasks as well as the engaging difference project. They may also feel accountable to constituents outside the project team, such as departmental superiors or colleagues.

These pressures make it imperative that leaders be prepared to support colleagues involved in Leveraging Difference work. That certainly means providing resources and social support when possible, but it's likely to mean offering political support as well. When people experiment with innovative solutions that may challenge the status quo, they sometimes need cover.

Perhaps the most powerful encouragement that leaders can offer, however, is their enthusiasm and their willingness to engage in the learning and development being undertaken by all those in the organization who are working with Leveraging Difference.

## No Simple Answers

Organizations don't fully develop a Leveraging Difference capability overnight. It would be tempting to think that you could work through this book and, at the end, find the "answer"—the right way to deal with diversity. Unfortunately (or fortunately), it will never be that simple.

On many occasions, I have worked with organizations or leaders who passionately wanted to make diversity work for them. And they would ask questions in the hope that I would be able to give them the comprehensive answers that would immediately solve their specific diversity dilemmas. I wish I could have given them the answers they wanted, but I couldn't. And I'm skeptical of anyone who says they have the prepackaged solution to all diversity problems.

There is no simple answer. As illustrated throughout this book, the best way to take advantage of the differences in an organization depends on that organization—its particular strategy, and its people, leadership, and systems—and the economic and social context in which it is operating.

## Key Takeaways

1. Leveraging Difference organizations fully utilize the capability in such a way that seeing, understanding, and engaging difference happen frequently and effortlessly. They become standard operating procedure.
2. Organizations transition to leveraging difference by capitalizing on the results of successful experimentation and continually "recycling" through the Leveraging Difference Cycle.
3. Leaders move organizations toward Leveraging Difference by working through the cycle relentlessly; encouraging their people to work through the cycle; communicating about the difference activities that have been put in place; and providing encouragement and energy to those involved in Leveraging Difference work.

# Epilogue

# The Power of the Margin

*Take from the margin to rethink the whole.*
*—Lani Guinier*

While I have critiqued Managing Diversity as an approach to dealing with difference, I haven't emphasized one of its strengths—an attribute that seems to be lacking in the Leveraging Difference frame. Managing Diversity was built to create change in a way that would provide access to members of groups that historically had been shut out. People of color, women, people with disabilities, people with LGBT orientations, and others with traditional differences were (and are) systematically discriminated against in this country. Managing Diversity efforts have helped close the gap in some areas, though disparities are still evident in hiring, development, and advancement. Contrary to the belief of some, we are not in a "post-racial" America, nor are we post–anything else. The enduring challenges of oppression and discrimination based on these differences will take time and effort to remedy. We must continue to engage such differences in order to create equity and justice for everyone.

I was following an online discussion board about sexual orientation and diversity not long ago, and the conversation turned toward the kinds of differences that leaders and organizations should worry about. One contributor was especially articulate in arguing that it is problematic to include cognitive diversity or skill diversity as part of real diversity work. If leaders and organizations allow themselves to focus too heavily on these differences, the argument unfolded, they will invariably divert attention away from the difficult challenges posed by traditional differences like race, gender, or sexual orientation. Those who want to define diversity more broadly are really "defining diversity out of existence," this individual asserted. "All equals nothing."

My worry is that leaders might read about Leveraging Difference and breathe a sigh of relief. They might be thinking, "Ah, here is a black man who is saying it's okay not to focus so heavily on race. And it's also okay not to focus on these other differences that are tough and intractable and controversial. Now we can just get back to work." I make no assumption that these individuals would be malicious, negligent, or ill willed in any way. I simply see them as leaders trying to manage many complex tasks and feeling relieved that one of the thorniest is taken off their plate, thanks to the Leveraging Difference rationale.

But if that were to happen, it would be a radical misreading of the text.

Leveraging Difference does not compromise important values and goals for equity and justice. Quite the contrary: it strongly reinforces them. In the introduction to this book, I shared a story about a group of executives who were discouraged by their CEO. When I made the comparison between their experience of disempowerment and that of African American employees, it was not coincidental that the group I referenced was black people. Disempowerment doesn't routinely happen to just anyone: there are differences that are particularly challenging, and I have found that to be so in every country I've visited or studied. In the United States, one of those challenging differences is race.

But that turns out to be good news.

When there are predictably intense dynamics surrounding a particular difference in a given cultural context (like race in the United States), learning how to navigate around that difference is often the best—and most efficient—way to develop a general Leveraging Difference capability. It offers an opportunity to see difference more clearly (for example, what are the differences within racial groups?). It provides tremendous opportunity for dialogue and experiences that deepen cross-difference understanding. A wide range of experiments could present themselves as a result. And don't worry: such inquiry will almost always have strategic implications. Labor markets, customer bases, and supplier markets are bound to include the given type of diversity and provide opportunities for value creation.

Intriguing discoveries can be made by focusing a Leveraging Difference process on one of the traditional differences. In working with one leader, a colleague and I challenged him with the paradox that in order to make progress in the career development of his African American employees, he had to stop focusing so much attention and so many resources on them. It sounded crazy at first. Stop focusing on the people who seemed to be struggling most? But we explained that the well-intentioned desire to support his black employees had the unintended effect of spotlighting them and creating even more organizational pressure for them to perform. That was actually causing their performance to diminish. The dynamics of differences aren't always obvious, but they can be learned.

At the core, wanting to do the right thing is admirable. But actually doing the right thing is ultimately much more important, and often much more challenging. By the way, there is no need to limit the "difference laboratory" to a focus on race. Similar benefits could result from doing a deep dive with any strategically relevant difference that also includes a legacy of systematic inequity. The point is that approaching these differences, not avoiding them, is the recipe for success.

## Taking from the Margin to Rethink the Whole

Compelling as the potential for learning about charged differences might be, that is not even the best reason to move toward them. I heard legal scholar Lani Guinier speak several years ago, and at the conclusion of her talk she encouraged her audience to "take from the margin to rethink the whole." I remember being struck by the comment; it made an impression on me, though at the time I didn't fully understand why. Having developed this work, I now understand better.

Leveraging Difference provides a mechanism for acknowledging and valuing the contribution of those who are not now and may never be mainstream. As a member of a minority group, I am familiar with the experience of being overlooked and undervalued. It's bad for the individual being overlooked. And often it's bad for a team or organization that is trying to achieve a goal of engaging and including its people. The marginal voice is the one that holds the seed of the next great idea, the next powerful invention. We can't create and innovate without the voice and vision that challenge our familiar and comfortable way of thinking and operating.

At MedTown, three separate insights led to the conclusion that touch screens were a good idea for the new distribution center. One subgroup learned that individuals with developmental disabilities work best with pictures and symbols. Another subgroup reported that steps in the processing of goods that required many keystrokes could be speeded up if they shifted to touchscreens. A third subgroup discovered that touchscreens caused fewer repetitive motion injuries for aging workers and that symbols were easier for them to see. As it turned out, once employees in the new distribution centers began using the touchscreen system, they agreed it was far superior to keyboards. Touchscreens were deployed to all of MedTown's distribution centers. Before this exploration, there was not enough collective insight to know the touchscreens were better. It was only in learning about the experiences of these different employees that the innovation took hold.

Consider the dramatic example of sidewalk ramps. As a result of the Americans with Disabilities Act of 1990, construction of sidewalk ramps was accelerated across the country. Those who couldn't easily navigate curbs, such as people in wheelchairs, were now afforded a means of access. Today virtually all public accessways include ramps. But if you observe who actually frequents these ramps, more often than not it's not wheelchair users. You're more likely to see bicyclists, parents pushing strollers, skateboarders, or people like me who are a little too lazy to lift my leg up over a curb. Responding to the requests of a marginal group generated an innovation that the larger society has embraced—so much so that it has led to yet more innovation. The profusion of ramps has made luggage on wheels a massively successful product. An accommodation made for a marginal group has benefited the larger community. Take from the margin to rethink the whole.

The promise of diversity is more profound than we might have imagined at first. Leaders lay the foundation for sustained excellence when they help create cultures that invite and embrace the contributions that emerge from diverse perspectives and backgrounds. From this dynamic diversity comes the next great idea, the breakthrough innovation, the community cohesiveness, and the commitment that can make a company extraordinary rather than merely ordinary.

# Notes

## Introduction: A New Possibility for Difference

1. Claire DeVeale and Lillian Manea, "Companies Embrace Power of Diversity," *Canadian HR Reporter*, December 17, 2007.
2. This example was more complex because the original voices of difference were also voices that were devalued within the organization. Social power and influence matter when it comes to determining which voices and which differences will be attended to.
3. William B. Johnston and A.E. Packer, *Workforce 2000: Work and Workers for the 21st Century* (Indianapolis, IN: Hudson Institute, 1987).
4. See the website www.northropgrumman.com/corporate-responsibility/diversity/diversity-vision-and-mission.html.
5. See PriceWaterhouseCoopers statement: www.pwc.com/us/en/about-us/diversity/pwc-diversity-commitment.jhtml.

## Chapter 1 The End of Diversity as We Know It

1. From the Chevron Corporation website (www.chevron.com).
2. Orlando C. Richard, "Racial Diversity, Business Strategy, and Firm Performance: A Resource-Based View," *Academy of Management Journal* 43, no. 2 (2000).
3. Thomas Kochan et al., "The Effects of Diversity on Business Performance: Report of the Diversity Research Network," *Human Resource Management* 42, no. 1 (2003).

4. Joshua M. Sacco and Neal Schmitt, "A Dynamic Multilevel Model of Demographic Diversity and Misfit Effects," *Journal of Applied Psychology* 90, no. 2 (2005).
5. S. Trevis Certo et al., "Top Management Teams, Strategy and Financial Performance: A Meta-Analytic Examination," *Journal of Management Studies* 43, no. 4 (2006).
6. Toyah Miller and María del Carmen Triana, "Demographic Diversity in the Boardroom: Mediators of the Board Diversity–Firm Performance Relationship," *Journal of Management Studies* 46, no. 5 (2009).
7. Orlando C. Richard, B. P. S. Murthi, and Kiran Ismail, "The Impact of Racial Diversity on Intermediate and Long-Term Performance: The Moderating Role of Environmental Context," *Strategic Management Journal* 28, no. 12 (2007).
8. Michele E. A. Jayne and Robert L. Dipboye, "Leveraging Diversity to Improve Business Performance: Research Findings and Recommendations for Organizations," *Human Resource Management* 43, no. 4 (2004).
9. Sujin K. Horwitz and Irwin B. Horwitz, "The Effects of Team Diversity on Team Outcomes: A Meta-Analytic Review of Team Demography," *Journal of Management* 33, no. 6 (2007).
10. Kathleen M. Eisenhardt and Behnam N. Tabrizi, "Accelerating Adaptive Processes: Product Innovation in the Global Computer Industry," *Administrative Science Quarterly* 40, no. 1 (1995).
11. Horwitz and Horwitz, "The Effects of Team Diversity on Team Outcomes."
12. Gordon W. Allport, *The Nature of Prejudice* (Cambridge: Addison-Wesley Publishing Co., 1954).
13. Jayne and Dipboye, "Leveraging Diversity to Improve Business Performance."
14. Anne S. Tsui, Terri D. Egan, and Charles A. O'Reilly III, "Being Different: Relational Demography and Organizational Attachment," *Administrative Science Quarterly* 37, no. 4 (1992).
15. Margery Weinstein, "Stymied by Diversity Hiring," *Training* 46, no. 3 (2009).
16. All disguised names of companies and individuals are marked with an asterisk in the text.
17. Carol T. Kulik, Loriann Roberson, and Elissa L. Perry, "The Multiple-Category Problem: Category Activation and Inhibition in the Hiring Process," *Academy of Management Review* 32, no. 2 (2007).

18. Marianne Bertrand and Sendhil Mullainathan, "Are Emily and Greg More Employable Than Lakisha and Jamal? A Field Experiment on Labor Market Discrimination," *The American Economic Review* 94, no. 4 (2004).
19. Robert P. Steel, Rodger W. Griffeth, and Peter W. Hom, "Practical Retention Policy for the Practical Manager," *Academy of Management Executive* 16, no. 2 (2002).
20. Patrick F. McKay et al., "Racial Differences in Employee Retention: Are Diversity Climate Perceptions the Key?" *Personnel Psychology* 60, no. 1 (2007).
21. Martin N. Davidson and Lynn Foster-Johnson, "Keeping Color in Corporate America: What Generates Organizational Commitment for Managers of Color," in *Darden Working Paper Series* (Charlottesville, VA: Darden Graduate School of Business, 2002).
22. Tsui, Egan, and O'Reilly, "Being Different: Relational Demography and Organizational Attachment."
23. Naomi Ellemers et al., "The Underrepresentation of Women in Science: Differential Commitment or the Queen Bee Syndrome?" *British Journal of Social Psychology* 43, no. 3 (2004).
24. Alexandra Kalev, Frank Dobbin, and Erin Kelly, "Best Practices or Best Guesses? Assessing the Efficacy of Corporate Affirmative Action and Diversity Policies," *American Sociological Review* 71, no. 4 (2006). In fact, some diversity training efforts were actually quite effective in creating desired change, and since 2002 even more effective training may be available. But according to this longitudinal research, it looks like more work is needed.
25. Aparna Joshi, Hui Liao, and Susan E. Jackson, "Cross-Level Effects of Workplace Diversity on Sales Performance and Pay," *Academy of Management Journal* 49, no. 3 (2006); and Richard, Murthi, and Ismail, "The Impact of Racial Diversity on Intermediate and Long-Term Performance."
26. Horwitz and Horwitz, "The Effects of Team Diversity on Team Outcomes: A Meta-Analytic Review of Team Demography."
27. Lisa Hope Pelled, Kathleen M. Eisenhardt, and Katherine R. Xin, "Exploring the Black Box: An Analysis of Work Group Diversity, Conflict, and Performance," *Administrative Science Quarterly* 44, no. 1 (1999).
28. Ellis Cose, *The Rage of a Privileged Class* (New York: HarperCollins, 1993); and Carol Pierce, David Wagner, and Bill Page, *A Male/Female Continuum: Paths to Colleagueship* (Laconia, NH: New Dynamics Press, 1995).

29. *Parr v. Woodmen of the World Life Insurance Company*, 791 F.2d 888 (1986).
30. Personal communication with legal counsel, May 2006.
31. David W. Pitts et al., "What Drives the Implementation of Diversity Management Programs? Evidence from Public Organizations," *Journal of Public Administration Research & Theory* 20, no. 4 (2010).
32. Jayne and Dipboye, "Leveraging Diversity to Improve Business Performance."
33. Ibid.
34. Martin N. Davidson and Karen L. Proudford, "Cycles of Resistance: How Dominants and Subordinants Collude to Undermine Diversity Efforts in Organizations," in *Diversity Resistance in Organizations,* ed. Kecia M. Thomas (New York: Lawrence Erlbaum Associates, 2008); and Angelo Falcón, "Latinos, Diversity, and Racial Fatigue in the Age of Obama," *National Civic Review* 98, no. 3 (2009).

### Chapter 2 The Beginning of Leveraging Difference

1. R. Richard Banks and Jennifer L. Eberhardt, "Social Psychological Processes and the Legal Bases of Racial Categorization," in Jennifer L. Eberhardt and Susan T. Fiske, eds., *Confronting Racism: The Problem and the Response* (Thousand Oaks, CA: Sage Publications, 1998).
2. Bob Baulch et al., "Ethnic Minority Development in Vietnam: A Socioeconomic Perspective," in *SSRN eLibrary* (World Bank Policy Research Working Paper 2836, 2002), http://ssrn.com/abstract=636183.
3. Ryan W. Quinn and Robert E. Quinn, *Lift: Becoming a Positive Force in Any Situation* (San Francisco: Berrett-Koehler Publishers, 2009).
4. Barry M. Staw, Lance E. Sandelands, and Jane E. Dutton, "Threat-Rigidity Effects in Organizational Behavior: A Multilevel Analysis," *Administrative Science Quarterly* 26, no. 4 (1981).
5. Sigal G. Barsade and Donald E. Gibson, "Why Does Affect Matter in Organizations?" *Academy of Management Perspectives* 21, no. 1 (2007).
6. Interview with the executive vice-president of a Fortune 500 clothing retailer, October 2010.
7. Data collected from fieldwork with a U.S. Fortune 100 chemical company.
8. Daan van Knippenberg and Michaéla C. Schippers, "Work Group Diversity," *Annual Review of Psychology* 58, no. 1 (2007).
9. Informal survey of a sample of 500 middle managers attending executive education or diversity leadership programs.

10. Kecia M. Thomas, ed., *Diversity Resistance in Organizations*, Applied Psychology Series (Hillsdale, NJ: Lawrence Erlbaum Associates, 2007).
11. Davidson and Proudford, "Cycles of Resistance."
12. Denise M. Rousseau and Snehal A. Tijoriwala, "What's a Good Reason to Change? Motivated Reasoning and Social Accounts in Promoting Organizational Change," *Journal of Applied Psychology* 84, no. 4 (1999).
13. Robin J. Ely and David A. Thomas, "Cultural Diversity at Work: The Effects of Diversity Perspectives on Work Group Processes and Outcomes," *Administrative Science Quarterly* 46, no. 2 (2001).
14. Rosabeth Moss Kanter, "Some Effects of Proportions on Group Life: Skewed Sex Ratios and Responses to Token Women," *American Journal of Sociology* 82, no. 5 (1977).


### Chapter 3 The Leveraging Difference Capability


1. Thomas L. Friedman, *The World Is Flat: A Brief History of the Twenty-First Century* (New York: Holtzbrinck Publishers, 2007).
2. This discussion draws heavily on Heather R. Wishik, Gerry Yemen, and Martin N. Davidson, *Wipro Technologies Europe* (Charlottesville, VA: Darden Business Publishing, 2002).


### Chapter 4 Seeing Difference


1. Lipi Patel and L. J. Bourgeois, "Note on Postmerger Integration" (Charlottesville, VA: Darden Business Publishing, 2009).
2. Sydney Finkelstein, "The DaimlerChrysler Merger," Tuck School of Business (Dartmouth) no. 1-0071, 2002, http://mba.tuck.dartmouth.edu/pdf/2002-1-0071.pdf (accessed May 31, 2011).
3. David P. Norton and James Coffey, "Building an Organized Process for Strategy Communication," *Harvard Business Publishing Newsletter* no. B0705A (2007).
4. Robert S. Kaplan and David P. Norton, *The Balanced Scorecard: Translating Strategy into Action* (Boston: Harvard Business School Press, 1996).
5. Robert S. Kaplan and David P. Norton, "Measuring the Strategic Readiness of Intangible Assets," *Harvard Business Review* 82, no. 2 (2004).
6. Yves Doz et al., "Diversity: The Key to Innovation Advantage," *European Business Forum*, April 1, 2004.

7. Leonard Greenhalgh, *Managing Strategic Relationships* (New York: The Free Press, 2001).
8. Kanter, "Some Effects of Proportions on Group Life."
9. Roy F. Baumeister, "Self-Esteem, Self-Presentation, and Future Interaction: A Dilemma of Reputation," *Journal of Personality* 50, no. 1 (1982).
10. Shelby Steele, *The Content of Our Character* (New York: St. Martin's Press, 1990).
11. Joel Brockner and Ted Hess, "Self-Esteem and Task Performance in Quality Circles," *Academy of Management Journal* 29, no. 3 (1986).
12. Jennifer Crocker et al., "Collective Self-Esteem and Psychological Well-Being among White, Black, and Asian College Students," *Personality & Social Psychology Bulletin* 20, no. 5 (1994).
13. Damian Stanley, Elizabeth Phelps, and Mahzarin Banaji, "The Neural Basis of Implicit Attitudes," *Current Directions in Psychological Science (Wiley-Blackwell)* 17, no. 2 (2008).
14. Anthony G. Greenwald and Mahzarin R. Banaji, "Implicit Social Cognition: Attitudes, Self-Esteem, and Stereotypes," *Psychological Review* 102, no. 1 (1995).
15. Malcolm Gladwell, *Blink: The Power of Thinking without Thinking* (Little, Brown and Co., 2005).
16. Eugene M. Caruso, Dobromir A. Rahnev, and Mahzarin R. Banaji, "Using Conjoint Analysis to Detect Discrimination: Revealing Covert Preferences from Overt Choices," *Social Cognition* 27, no. 1 (2009).
17. Thomas F. Pettigrew and Linda R. Tropp, "A Meta-Analytic Test of Intergroup Contact Theory," *Journal of Personality and Social Psychology* 90, no. 5 (2006).
18. Ibid.
19. Steven G. Young and Heather M. Claypool, "Mere Exposure Has Differential Effects on Attention Allocation to Threatening and Neutral Stimuli," *Journal of Experimental Social Psychology* 46, no. 2 (2010).
20. Pierce, Wagner, and Page, *A Male/Female Continuum.*
21. Rhiannon N. Turner and Richard J. Crisp, "Imagining Intergroup Contact Reduces Implicit Prejudice," *British Journal of Social Psychology* 49, no. 1 (2010).

## Chapter 5 Understanding Difference

1. American Institute of Certified Public Accountants, "A Decade of Changes in the Profession: Workforce Trends and Human Capital

Practices," in *AICPA Work/Life and Women's Initiatives 2004 Research* (2004).

2. Alice H. Eagly and Linda L. Carli, "The Female Leadership Advantage: An Evaluation of the Evidence," *Leadership Quarterly* 14, no. 6 (2003).
3. Gal Raz, Gerry Yemen, and Martin N. Davidson, "Kulicke & Soffa Industries Inc. in China: Transferring Knowledge (A)" (Charlottesville, VA: Darden Business Publishing, 2010).
4. Jordan A. Litman, "Curiosity and the Pleasures of Learning: Wanting and Liking New Information," *Cognition & Emotion* 19, no. 6 (2005).
5. George Loewenstein, "The Psychology of Curiosity: A Review and Reinterpretation," *Psychological Bulletin* 116, no. 1 (1994).
6. Ibid.
7. Peter M. Senge, *The Fifth Discipline: The Art and Practice of the Learning Organization* (New York: Doubleday, 1990).
8. V. Jean Ramsey and Jean Kantambu Latting, "A Typology of Intergroup Competencies," *Journal of Applied Behavioral Science* 41, no. 3 (2005).
9. Charles H. Tardy and Kathryn Dindia, "Self-Disclosure: Strategic Revelation of Information in Personal and Professional Relationships," in *The Handbook of Communication Skills* (3rd ed.), ed. Owen Hargie (New York: Routledge, 2006).
10. Elizabeth Wolfe Morrison and Frances J. Milliken, "Organizational Silence: A Barrier to Change and Development in a Pluralistic World," *Academy of Management Review* 25, no. 4 (2000).
11. Robin Ely, Debra Meyerson, and Martin N. Davidson, "Rethinking Political Correctness," *Harvard Business Review* 84, no. 9 (2006).
12. Ibid.
13. Kirk Warren Brown and Richard M. Ryan, "The Benefits of Being Present: Mindfulness and Its Role in Psychological Well-Being," *Journal of Personality & Social Psychology* 84, no. 4 (2003).
14. Kirk Warren Brown, Richard M. Ryan, and J. David Creswell, "Mindfulness: Theoretical Foundations and Evidence for Its Salutary Effects," *Psychological Inquiry* 18, no. 4 (2007).
15. Richard M. Ryan and Edward L. Deci, "Autonomy Is No Illusion: Self-Determination Theory and the Empirical Study of Authenticity, Awareness, and Will," in *Handbook of Experimental Existential Psychology.*, ed. Jeff Greenberg, Sander L. Koole, and Tom Pyszczynski (New York: Guilford Press, 2004).

16. Michel Girodo, "Self-Talk: Mechanisms in Anxiety and Stress Management," in *Stress and Anxiety*, ed. Charles D. Spielberger and Irwin G. Sarason (Oxford: Hemisphere, 1977).
17. Kate G. Niederhoffer and James W. Pennebaker, "Sharing One's Story: On the Benefits of Writing or Talking About Emotional Experience," in *Oxford Handbook of Positive Psychology* (2nd ed.), ed. Shane J. Lopez and C. R. Snyder, Oxford Library of Psychology (New York: Oxford University Press, 2009).
18. Clyde E. Witt, "Design for Diversity," *Material Handling Management*, June 1, 2007.
19. Bridge Partners LLC, "Q&A with Kerrie Peraino, VP Human Resources, Chief Diversity Officer, American Express," *Insights,* April 2011 (http://www.bridgepartnersllc.com/Newsletters/2011-April.pdf).
20. Personal communication, 2000.
21. Personal communication, 2007.
22. Martin N. Davidson and Gerry Yemen, "Diversity at JPMorgan Chase: Right Is Good Enough for Me" (Charlottesville, VA: Darden Business Publishing, 2009).
23. Donna Chrobot-Mason, Rosemary Hays-Thomas, and Heather Wishik, "Understanding and Defusing Resistance to Diversity Training and Learning," in *Diversity Resistance in Organizations*, ed. Kecia M. Thomas, Series in Applied Psychology (New York: Lawrence Erlbaum Associates, 2008).
24. Peggy McIntosh, "White Privilege: Unpacking the Invisible Knapsack," in *Re-Visioning Family Therapy: Race, Culture, and Gender in Clinical Practice*, ed. Monica McGoldrick (New York: Guilford Press, 1998); and Jim Sidanius and Felicia Pratto, *Social Dominance: An Intergroup Theory of Social Hierarchy and Oppression* (Cambridge: Cambridge University Press, 1999).
25. Caletha Crawford, "Multicultural Approach Charts Future of the Beauty Business," *AtlantaPost.com* (July 8, 2010), http://atlanta-post.com/2010/07/08/a-new-multicultural-approach-charts-the-future-of-the-beauty-businessbccrawford/.
26. Galen V. Bodenhausen, "Diversity in the Person, Diversity in the Group: Challenges of Identity Complexity for Social Perception and Social Interaction," *European Journal of Social Psychology* 40, no. 1 (2010).
27. Martin N. Davidson and Heather R. Wishik, "Learning to Lead: Some Impacts of Social Identity on Management and Leadership Development," in *Darden Working Paper Series* (Charlottesville, VA: Darden Graduate School of Business, 2002).

28. William Duggan, *Strategic Intuition: The Creative Spark in Human Achievement* (New York: Columbia University Press, 2007).

## Chapter 6 Engaging Difference

1. George P. Huber, "Organizational Learning: The Contributing Processes and the Literatures," *Organization Science* 2, no. 1 (1991).
2. James C. Collins and Jerry I. Porras, "Building Your Company's Vision," *Harvard Business Review* 74, no. 5 (1996).
3. Michael Beer, Russell A. Eisenstat, and Bert Spector, "Why Change Programs Don't Produce Change," *Harvard Business Review* 68, no. 6 (1990); and John P. Kotter, *Leading Change* (Boston, MA: Harvard Business School Press, 1996).
4. Kotter, *Leading Change.*
5. Tamara L. Friedrich et al., "Leading for Innovation: Reevaluating Leader Influences on Innovation with Regard to Innovation Type and Complexity," *International Studies of Management & Organization* 40, no. 2 (2010).
6. Teresa M. Amabile and Mukti Khaire, "Creativity and the Role of the Leader," *Harvard Business Review* 86, no. 10 (2008).
7. Umpqua Bank case drawn from Cynthia Barton Rabe, "How Leaders Use Zero-Gravity Thinkers to Stimulate Innovation," *Strategy & Leadership* 34, no. 6 (2006).

## Chapter 7 Becoming a Leveraging Difference Organization

1. DeVeale and Manea, "Companies Embrace Power of Diversity," www.proquest.com/.
2. Ibid.
3. Ariel Education Initiative, "401(K) Plans in Living Color: A Study of 401(K) Savings Disparities across Racial and Ethnic Groups" (Ariel Investments and Hewitt Associates, 2008).
4. DeVeale and Manea, "Companies Embrace Power of Diversity."
5. Sigal G. Barsade, "The Ripple Effect: Emotional Contagion and Its Influence on Group Behavior," *Administrative Science Quarterly* 47, no. 4 (2002).

# Bibliography

Allport, Gordon W. *The Nature of Prejudice*. Cambridge: Addison-Wesley Publishing Co., 1954.

Amabile, Teresa M., and Mukti Khaire. "Creativity and the Role of the Leader." *Harvard Business Review* 86, no. 10 (2008): 100–109.

American Institute of Certified Public Accountants. "A Decade of Changes in the Profession: Workforce Trends and Human Capital Practices." In *AICPA Work/Life and Women's Initiatives 2004 Research*, 2004.

Ariel Education Initiative. "401(K) Plans in Living Color: A Study of 401(K) Savings Disparities across Racial and Ethnic Groups," 21. Ariel Investments and Hewitt Associates, 2008.

Banks, R. Richard, and Jennifer L. Eberhardt. "Social Psychological Processes and the Legal Bases of Racial Categorization." In *Confronting Racism: The Problem and the Response*, edited by Jennifer L. Eberhardt and Susan T. Fiske, 54–75. Thousand Oaks, CA: Sage Publications, 1998.

Barsade, Sigal G. "The Ripple Effect: Emotional Contagion and Its Influence on Group Behavior." *Administrative Science Quarterly* 47, no. 4 (2002): 644–75.

Barsade, Sigal G., and Donald E. Gibson. "Why Does Affect Matter in Organizations?" *Academy of Management Perspectives* 21, no. 1 (2007): 36–59.

Baulch, Bob, Dominique Haughton, Jonathan H. Haughton, and Truong Thi Kim Chuyen. "Ethnic Minority Development in Vietnam: A Socioeconomic Perspective." In *SSRN eLibrary*, World Bank Policy Research Working Paper 2836 (2002), http://ssrn.com/abstract=636183.

Beer, Michael, Russell A. Eisenstat, and Bert Spector. "Why Change Programs Don't Produce Change." *Harvard Business Review* 68, no. 6 (1990): 158–66.

Bertrand, Marianne, and Sendhil Mullainathan. "Are Emily and Greg More Employable Than Lakisha and Jamal? A Field Experiment on Labor Market Discrimination." *The American Economic Review* 94, no. 4 (2004): 991–1013.

Bodenhausen, Galen V. "Diversity in the Person, Diversity in the Group: Challenges of Identity Complexity for Social Perception and Social Interaction." *European Journal of Social Psychology* 40, no. 1 (2010): 1–16.

Bridge Partners LLC. "Q&A with Kerrie Peraino, VP Human Resources, Chief Diversity Officer, American Express." *Insights* (April 2011): 4–5, http://www.bridgepartnersllc.com/Newsletters/2011-April.pdf.

Brockner, Joel, and Ted Hess. "Self-Esteem and Task Performance in Quality Circles." *Academy of Management Journal* 29, no. 3 (1986): 617–23.

Brown, Kirk Warren, and Richard M. Ryan. "The Benefits of Being Present: Mindfulness and Its Role in Psychological Well-Being." *Journal of Personality & Social Psychology* 84, no. 4 (2003): 822–48.

Brown, Kirk Warren, Richard M. Ryan, and J. David Creswell. "Mindfulness: Theoretical Foundations and Evidence for Its

Salutary Effects." *Psychological Inquiry* 18, no. 4 (2007): 211–37.

Caruso, Eugene M., Dobromir A. Rahnev, and Mahzarin R. Banaji. "Using Conjoint Analysis to Detect Discrimination: Revealing Covert Preferences from Overt Choices." *Social Cognition* 27, no. 1 (2009): 128–37.

Certo, S. Trevis, Richard H. Lester, Catherine M. Dalton, and Dan R. Dalton. "Top Management Teams, Strategy and Financial Performance: A Meta-Analytic Examination." *Journal of Management Studies* 43, no. 4 (2006): 813–39.

Chrobot-Mason, Donna, Rosemary Hays-Thomas, and Heather Wishik. "Understanding and Defusing Resistance to Diversity Training and Learning." In *Diversity Resistance in Organizations*, Series in Applied Psychology, edited by Kecia M. Thomas, 23–54. New York: Lawrence Erlbaum Associates, 2008.

Collins, James C., and Jerry I. Porras. "Building Your Company's Vision." *Harvard Business Review* 74, no. 5 (1996): 65–77.

Cose, Ellis. *The Rage of a Privileged Class*. New York: Harper Collins, 1993.

Crocker, Jennifer, Riia Luhtanen, Bruce Blaine, and Stephanie Broadnax. "Collective Self-Esteem and Psychological Well-Being among White, Black, and Asian College Students." *Personality & Social Psychology Bulletin* 20, no. 5 (1994): 503–13.

Davidson, Martin N., and Lynn Foster-Johnson. "Keeping Color in Corporate America: What Generates Organizational Commitment for Managers of Color." In *Darden Working Paper Series*, 1–29, Darden Graduate School of Business, University of Virginia, Charlottesville, VA, 2002.

Davidson, Martin N., and Karen L. Proudford. "Cycles of Resistance: How Dominants and Subordinants Collude to Undermine Diversity Efforts in Organizations." In *Diversity Resistance in Organizations: Manifestations and Solutions*, edited by Kecia M. Thomas, 249–72. Hillsdale, NJ: Lawrence Erlbaum Associates, 2007.

Davidson, Martin N., and Heather R. Wishik. "Learning to Lead: Some Impacts of Social Identity on Management and Leadership Development." In *Darden Working Paper Series*, 1–38. Darden Graduate School of Business, University of Virginia, Charlottesville, VA, 2002.

Davidson, Martin N., and Gerry Yemen. "Diversity at JPMorgan Chase: Right Is Good Enough for Me." Charlottesville, VA: Darden Business Publishing, 2009.

DeVeale, Claire, and Lillian Manea. "Companies Embrace Power of Diversity." *Canadian HR Reporter* (December 17, 2007): 14–15.

Doz, Yves, Jose Santos, Peter Williamson, and Franklin Berrebi. "Diversity: The Key to Innovation Advantage." *European Business Forum* (April 1, 2004): 25–27.

Duggan, William. *Strategic Intuition: The Creative Spark in Human Achievement*. New York: Columbia University Press, 2007.

Eagly, Alice H., and Linda L. Carli. "The Female Leadership Advantage: An Evaluation of the Evidence." *Leadership Quarterly* 14, no. 6 (2003): 807.

Eisenhardt, Kathleen M., and Behnam N. Tabrizi. "Accelerating Adaptive Processes: Product Innovation in the Global Computer Industry." *Administrative Science Quarterly* 40, no. 1 (1995): 84–110.

Ellemers, Naomi, Henriette Van Den Heuvel, Dick de Gilder, Anne Maass, and Alessandra Bonvini. "The Underrepresentation of Women in Science: Differential Commitment or the Queen Bee Syndrome?" *British Journal of Social Psychology* 43, no. 3 (2004): 315–38.

Ely, Robin J., and David A. Thomas. "Cultural Diversity at Work: The Effects of Diversity Perspectives on Work Group Processes and Outcomes." *Administrative Science Quarterly* 46, no. 2 (2001): 229–73.

Ely, Robin, Debra Meyerson, and Martin N. Davidson. "Rethinking Political Correctness." *Harvard Business Review* 84, no. 9 (2006): 79-87.

Fagenson, Ellen A., ed. *Women in Management: Trends, Issues, and Challenges in Managerial Diversity*, Women and Work: A Research and Policy Series, vol. 4. Newbury Park, CA: Sage Publications, 1993.

Falcón, Angelo. "Latinos, Diversity, and Racial Fatigue in the Age of Obama." *National Civic Review* 98, no. 3 (2009): 40–42.

Friedman, Thomas L. *The World Is Flat: A Brief History of the Twenty-First Century*. New York: Holtzbrinck Publishers, 2007.

Friedrich, Tamara L., Michael D. Mumford, Brandon Vessey, Cheryl K. Beeler, and Dawn L. Eubanks. "Leading for Innovation: Reevaluating Leader Influences on Innovation with Regard to Innovation Type and Complexity." *International Studies of Management & Organization* 40, no. 2 (2010): 6–29.

Girodo, Michel. "Self-Talk: Mechanisms in Anxiety and Stress Management." In *Stress and Anxiety*, edited by Charles D. Spielberger and Irwin G. Sarason, 229–50. Oxford: Hemisphere, 1977.

Gladwell, Malcolm. *Blink: The Power of Thinking without Thinking*. New York: Little, Brown and Co., 2005.

Greenhalgh, Leonard. *Managing Strategic Relationships*. New York: The Free Press, 2001.

Greenwald, Anthony G., and Mahzarin R. Banaji. "Implicit Social Cognition: Attitudes, Self-Esteem, and Stereotypes." *Psychological Review* 102, no. 1 (1995): 4–27.

Horwitz, Sujin K., and Irwin B. Horwitz. "The Effects of Team Diversity on Team Outcomes: A Meta-Analytic Review of Team

Demography." *Journal of Management* 33, no. 6 (2007): 987–1015.

Huber, George P. "Organizational Learning: The Contributing Processes and the Literatures." *Organization Science* 2, no. 1 (1991): 88–115.

Jayne, Michele E. A., and Robert L. Dipboye. "Leveraging Diversity to Improve Business Performance: Research Findings and Recommendations for Organizations." *Human Resource Management* 43, no. 4 (2004): 409–24.

Joshi, Aparna, Hui Liao, and Susan E. Jackson. "Cross-Level Effects of Workplace Diversity on Sales Performance and Pay." *Academy of Management Journal* 49, no. 3 (2006): 459–81.

Kalev, Alexandra, Frank Dobbin, and Erin Kelly. "Best Practices or Best Guesses? Assessing the Efficacy of Corporate Affirmative Action and Diversity Policies." *American Sociological Review* 71, no. 4 (2006): 589–617.

Kanter, Rosabeth Moss. "Some Effects of Proportions on Group Life: Skewed Sex Ratios and Responses to Token Women." *American Journal of Sociology* 82, no. 5 (1977): 965–90.

Kaplan, Robert S., and David P. Norton. *The Balanced Scorecard: Translating Strategy into Action*. Boston: Harvard Business School Press, 1996.

———. "Measuring the Strategic Readiness of Intangible Assets." *Harvard Business Review* 82, no. 2 (2004): 52–63.

Kochan, Thomas, Katerina Bezrukova, Robin Ely, Susan Jackson, Aparna Joshi, Karen Jehn, Jonathan Leonard, David Levine, and David Thomas. "The Effects of Diversity on Business Performance: Report of the Diversity Research Network." *Human Resource Management* 42, no. 1 (2003): 3–21.

Kotter, John P. *Leading Change*. Boston: Harvard Business School Press, 1996.

Kulik, Carol T., Loriann Roberson, and Elissa L. Perry. "The Multiple-Category Problem: Category Activation and Inhibition in the Hiring Process." *Academy of Management Review* 32, no. 2 (2007): 529–48.

Litman, Jordan A. "Curiosity and the Pleasures of Learning: Wanting and Liking New Information." *Cognition & Emotion* 19, no. 6 (2005): 793–814.

Loewenstein, George. "The Psychology of Curiosity: A Review and Reinterpretation." *Psychological Bulletin* 116, no. 1 (1994): 75–98.

McIntosh, Peggy. "White Privilege: Unpacking the Invisible Knapsack." In *Re-Visioning Family Therapy: Race, Culture, and Gender in Clinical Practice*, edited by Monica McGoldrick, 147–52. New York: Guilford Press, 1998.

McKay, Patrick F., Derek R. Avery, Scott Toniandel, Mark A. Morris, Morela Hernandez, and Michelle R. Hebl. "Racial Differences in Employee Retention: Are Diversity Climate Perceptions the Key?" *Personnel Psychology* 60, no. 1 (2007): 35–62.

Miller, Toyah, and María del Carmen Triana. "Demographic Diversity in the Boardroom: Mediators of the Board Diversity–Firm Performance Relationship." *Journal of Management Studies* 46, no. 5 (2009): 755–86.

Morrison, Elizabeth Wolfe, and Frances J. Milliken. "Organizational Silence: A Barrier to Change and Development in a Pluralistic World." *Academy of Management Review* 25, no. 4 (2000): 706–25.

Niederhoffer, Kate G., and James W. Pennebaker. "Sharing One's Story: On the Benefits of Writing or Talking About Emotional Experience." In *Oxford Handbook of Positive* Psychology (2nd ed.), edited by Shane J. Lopez and C. R. Snyder, 621–32. Oxford Library of Psychology. New York: Oxford University Press, 2009.

Norton, David P., and James Coffey. "Building an Organized Process for Strategy Communication." *Harvard Business Publishing Newsletter*, no. B0705A (May 15, 2007): 3-7.

*Parr v. Woodmen of the World Life Insurance Company*, 791 F.2d 888 (1986).

Patel, Lipi, and L. J. Bourgeois. "Note on Postmerger Integration." Charlottesville, VA: Darden Business Publishing, 2009.

Pelled, Lisa Hope, Kathleen M. Eisenhardt, and Katherine R. Xin. "Exploring the Black Box: An Analysis of Work Group Diversity, Conflict, and Performance." *Administrative Science Quarterly* 44, no. 1 (1999): 1–28.

Pettigrew, Thomas F., and Linda R. Tropp. "A Meta-Analytic Test of Intergroup Contact Theory." *Journal of Personality and Social Psychology* 90, no. 5 (2006): 751–83.

Pierce, Carol, David Wagner, and Bill Page. *A Male/Female Continuum: Paths to Colleagueship*. Laconia, NH: New Dynamics Press, 1995.

Pitts, David W., Alisa K. Hicklin, Daniel P. Hawes, and Erin Melton. "What Drives the Implementation of Diversity Management Programs? Evidence from Public Organizations." *Journal of Public Administration Research & Theory* 20, no. 4 (2010): 867–86.

Quinn, Ryan W., and Robert E. Quinn. *Lift: Becoming a Positive Force in Any Situation*. San Francisco: Berrett-Koehler Publishers, 2009.

Rabe, Cynthia Barton. "How Leaders Use Zero-Gravity Thinkers to Stimulate Innovation." *Strategy & Leadership* 34, no. 6 (2006): 38–43.

Ramsey, V. Jean, and Jean Kantambu Latting. "A Typology of Intergroup Competencies." *Journal of Applied Behavioral Science* 41, no. 3 (2005): 265–84.

Raz, Gal, Gerry Yemen, and Martin N. Davidson. "Kulicke & Soffa Industries Inc. in China: Transferring Knowledge (A)." Charlottesville, VA: Darden Business Publishing, 2010.

Richard, Orlando C. "Racial Diversity, Business Strategy, and Firm Performance: A Resource-Based View." *Academy of Management Journal* 43, no. 2 (2000): 164–77.

Richard, Orlando C., B. P. S. Murthi, and Kiran Ismail. "The Impact of Racial Diversity on Intermediate and Long-Term Performance: The Moderating Role of Environmental Context." *Strategic Management Journal* 28, no. 12 (2007): 1213–33.

Rousseau, Denise M., and Snehal A. Tijoriwala. "What's a Good Reason to Change? Motivated Reasoning and Social Accounts in Promoting Organizational Change." *Journal of Applied Psychology* 84, no. 4 (1999): 514–28.

Ryan, Richard M., and Edward L. Deci. "Autonomy Is No Illusion: Self-Determination Theory and the Empirical Study of Authenticity, Awareness, and Will." In *Handbook of Experimental Existential Psychology*, edited by Jeff Greenberg, Sander L. Koole and Tom Pyszczynski, 449–79. New York: Guilford Press, 2004.

Sacco, Joshua M., and Neal Schmitt. "A Dynamic Multilevel Model of Demographic Diversity and Misfit Effects." *Journal of Applied Psychology* 90, no. 2 (2005): 203–31.

Senge, Peter M. *The Fifth Discipline: The Art and Practice of the Learning Organization.* New York: Doubleday, 1990.

Sidanius, Jim, and Felicia Pratto. *Social Dominance: An Intergroup Theory of Social Hierarchy and Oppression.* Cambridge: Cambridge University Press, 1999.

Stanley, Damian, Elizabeth Phelps, and Mahzarin Banaji. "The Neural Basis of Implicit Attitudes." *Current Directions in Psychological Science (Wiley-Blackwell)* 17, no. 2 (2008): 164–70.

Staw, Barry M., Lance E. Sandelands, and Jane E. Dutton. "Threat-Rigidity Effects in Organizational Behavior: A Multilevel Analysis." *Administrative Science Quarterly* 26, no. 4 (1981): 501–24.

Steel, Robert P., Rodger W. Griffeth, and Peter W. Hom. "Practical Retention Policy for the Practical Manager." *Academy of Management Executive* 16, no. 2 (2002): 149–62.

Steele, Shelby. *The Content of Our Character.* New York: St. Martin's Press, 1990.

Tardy, Charles H., and Kathryn Dindia. "Self-Disclosure: Strategic Revelation of Information in Personal and Professional Relationships." In *The Handbook of Communication Skills* (3rd ed.), edited by Owen Hargie, 229–66. New York: Routledge, 2006.

Thomas, Kecia M., ed. *Diversity Resistance in Organizations: Manifestations and Solutions.* Series in Applied Psychology. Hillsdale, NJ: Lawrence Erlbaum Associates, 2007.

Tsui, Anne S., Terri D. Egan, and Charles A. O'Reilly III. "Being Different: Relational Demography and Organizational Attachment." *Administrative Science Quarterly* 37, no. 4 (1992): 549–79.

Turner, Rhiannon N., and Richard J. Crisp. "Imagining Intergroup Contact Reduces Implicit Prejudice." *British Journal of Social Psychology* 49, no. 1 (2010): 129–42.

Van Knippenberg, Daan, and Michaéla C. Schippers. "Work Group Diversity." *Annual Review of Psychology* 58, no. 1 (2007): 515–41.

Weinstein, Margery. "Stymied by Diversity Hiring." *Training* 46, no. 3 (2009): 1.

Wishik, Heather R., Gerry Yemen, and Martin N. Davidson. "Wipro Technologies Europe (A)." Charlottesville, VA: Darden Business Publishing, 2002.

———. "Wipro Technologies Europe (B)." Charlottesville, VA: Darden Business Publishing, 2002.

———. "Wipro Technologies Europe (C)." Charlottesville, VA: Darden Business Publishing, 2002.

Witt, Clyde E. "Design for Diversity." *Material Handling Management*, June 1, 2007: 32, 34, 36.

Young, Steven G., and Heather M. Claypool. "Mere Exposure Has Differential Effects on Attention Allocation to Threatening and Neutral Stimuli." *Journal of Experimental Social Psychology* 46, no. 2 (2010): 424–27.

# Index

# Acknowledgments

This book is the fruit of many people's labor. First I must thank my friend, colleague, and co-author Heather R. Wishik. For nearly twenty years, we have worked together consulting, conducting research, writing cases, and teaching about diversity and global leadership. Much of the insight for this book is the product of our many collaborations and conversations about what we were learning in our work and in our lives as we crossed boundaries of difference. Heather and I co-authored three of the chapters of this book, and her feedback on early drafts was invaluable.

I am indebted to my scholar colleagues who collaborated with me on research and writing connected to this book. And as I crafted these acknowledgments, I could not separate collaboration on work from colleagueship and friendship. So I thank my professional family: Charles Behling, Ella Bell, Taylor Cox, Robin Ely, Bernardo Ferdman, Lynn Foster-Johnson, Ray Friedman, Leonard Greenhalgh, Terry de Guzman, Erika James, Joanne Martin, Debra Meyerson, Stella Nkomo, Elizabeth Powell, Karen Proudford, Marian Ruderman, and David Thomas. My students and research assistants were incredibly helpful throughout, and I am grateful to them: Riwa Akiyama, Bret Crane, Alex Forrest, Janine Hum, and Jaime Maldonado. I also thank the Darden Graduate School of Business at the University of Virginia and the Batten Institute for their generous funding in support of this research.

The insights in this book didn't hatch whole from my ivory-tower experience. They were honed in my relationships with gifted leaders in organizations all over the world. I am grateful to many key figures who rolled up their sleeves and invited me to help tackle these issues in their organizations. I am indebted to Decker Anstrom, Kathy Auerbach, Frank Batten, Jr., Ted Bell, J. Ted Childs, Felix Davis, Jaime Dimon, Christopher DuPuy, Rosanna Durruthy, Grace Figueredo, Debbie Gentry, Keith Henry, Charlie Hill, Mona Lau, Erin Magnuson, Greg Mech, Ron Meraz, Colbert Narcisse, Ossie Reid, Suzanne Richards, Mike Riley, Todd Sears, Mark Settles, Phil Sieg, Claiborne Smith, Margaret Watson, Claudette Whiting, Darlene Williams, and Claudine Young. I also thank the hundreds of executives I've had the privilege to work with in conjunction with the Darden Executive Education Program.

I'm very appreciative of the support I have received from my colleagues at the Darden School and the University of Virginia. I thank my deans Robert Bruner, Robert Harris, and Ted Snyder for their leadership and support. I also thank my wonderful faculty and staff colleagues for their support (even when they didn't know they were helping me): Jay Bourgeois, Jim Clawson, Greg Fairchild, Jim Freeland, Paul Harper, Alec Horniman, Wendy Huber, Lynn Isabella, Jeanne Liedtka, David Newkirk, Anton Ovchinnikov, Bobby Parmar, Ryan Quinn, Gal Raz, Kellie Sauls, Scott Snell, Melissa Thomas-Hunt, Jack Weber, and Sarah Wilcox-Elliott. Gerry Yemen was an especially valued colleague in helping me to conduct interviews and craft case studies, some of which appear in this book. And I could not have handled my day-to-day work had it not been for my friend and outstanding assistant, Lynne Lambert.

I began my practical work in the field of diversity when I had the privilege to attend a five-day multicultural workshop as a guest of DuPont back in the early 1990s. From that point on, I joined an outstanding network of consultants who have become my colleagues, teachers, and friends. I am grateful to Barbara Berry, Janice Eddy, Tim Ewing, Ron Gibson, Evangelina Holvino, Rick Huntley, Cecy Kuruvilla, Ann Akiko Kusumoto, Rianna Moore, the late Richard Orange, Bill Page, Anita Sanchez, Kit Tennis, Sharon Bueno Washington, Joseph Wheeler, and Heather Wishik.

I owe a tremendous debt to my friends and mentors at Learning as Leadership, a U.S.-based leadership development organization, in whose seminars my colleagues and I participated. The work I was able do with the entire team was essential in enabling me to see possibilities for this work. I am especially grateful to Marc-Andre Olivier, Lara Nuer, Shayne Hughes, Noah Nuer, Nathalie Salles, LeeAnn Mallorie, and every member of the LaL team. I also thank the many friends I met in the LaL network, with whom I learned so much about differences.

I offer a special thanks to my friend, college roommate, author, and rock star (no, he actually *is* a rock star) Jacob Slichter. His support when I couldn't figure out how to string two words together inspired me and helped me get this done. I also thank my longtime friends and advisors Reginald Hudlin and Craig Preston who got me thinking in interesting ways and who just kept sending vibes of support at all the right times.

This book exists because of the team at Berrett-Koehler Publishers. I am especially grateful to my editors Neal Maillet and Jeevan

Sivasubramaniam, and to reviewers and colleagues who provided extremely valuable feedback on early drafts: James Collier, Danielle Goodman, Jeff Kulick, and Tamara Schweitzer. Connie Glover continues to be an incredible partner in the development, expression, and marketing of my work. Christine Davis was most helpful in copyediting early drafts.

I cannot fully convey how much the support of my family meant throughout this process. My big brothers Gary Davidson and Arlando Davidson are, well, my big brothers. I could do very little without them in my life. Without the love and support they've given me throughout my life, there's no me.

I am most indebted to my beloved wife and partner, Rachel L. Bagby. When we met twenty-eight years ago it was love at first sight, but I had no idea how deep that could run. The book is hers as well. This work has emerged and I have emerged because of our relationship these many years. And that's that.

# About the Author

Christopher Bond Photography

**Dr. Martin N. Davidson** is Associate Professor of Leadership and Organizational Behavior at the Darden Graduate School of Business, University of Virginia, and also recently completed a three-year appointment as Associate Dean and Chief Diversity Officer for the School. In his research, teaching, and consulting, Martin focuses on how leaders can use diversity strategically to create sustainable competitive advantages for their firms, both globally and domestically. His research on the impact of culture and ethnicity on career development and on conflict management is featured in top managerial and academic publications, including *Harvard Business Review, Administrative Science Quarterly, Research on Negotiation in Organizations,* and the *International Journal of Conflict Management*. His work also appears in cutting-edge books such as *Diversity Resistance in Organizations: Manifestations and Solutions* and *Exploring Positive Relationships at Work*. He has conducted research on four continents identifying the critical competencies for managing effectively across national boundaries.

He consults with a host of Fortune 100 firms, as well as government agencies, and nonprofit organizations. He also teaches leadership in Darden's MBA and Executive Leadership programs. Martin was elected chair of the Gender and Diversity in Organizations Division of the Academy of Management for 2006–2007. He has been featured in numerous media outlets, including *The New York Times*, *BusinessWeek*, *The Wall Street Journal*, *The Washington Post*, National Public Radio, and Minnesota Public Radio. His contributions to WashingtonPost.com's "On Leadership" series have been featured in print as well as online.

Before Martin joined the Darden faculty in 1998, he was a member of the Leadership faculty of the Tuck School of Business Administration at Dartmouth College. He earned his PhD at Stanford University and his AB at Harvard University. He is a native of Cleveland, Ohio, where his extended family still resides. Martin enjoys playing his upright bass and spending time with his wife, Rachel Bagby, on their solar-powered farm in Virginia. For more information about Martin N. Davidson and his research, and to view his weekly blog, "In My Opinion," visit www.leveragingdifference.com.

# Berrett–Koehler Publishers

**Berrett-Koehler** is an independent publisher dedicated to an ambitious mission: *Creating a World That Works for All.*

We believe that to truly create a better world, action is needed at all levels—individual, organizational, and societal. At the individual level, our publications help people align their lives with their values and with their aspirations for a better world. At the organizational level, our publications promote progressive leadership and management practices, socially responsible approaches to business, and humane and effective organizations. At the societal level, our publications advance social and economic justice, shared prosperity, sustainability, and new solutions to national and global issues.

A major theme of our publications is "Opening Up New Space." Berrett-Koehler titles challenge conventional thinking, introduce new ideas, and foster positive change. Their common quest is changing the underlying beliefs, mindsets, institutions, and structures that keep generating the same cycles of problems, no matter who our leaders are or what improvement programs we adopt.

We strive to practice what we preach—to operate our publishing company in line with the ideas in our books. At the core of our approach is stewardship, which we define as a deep sense of responsibility to administer the company for the benefit of all of our "stakeholder" groups: authors, customers, employees, investors, service providers, and the communities and environment around us.

We are grateful to the thousands of readers, authors, and other friends of the company who consider themselves to be part of the "BK Community." We hope that you, too, will join us in our mission.

**A BK Business Book**

This book is part of our BK Business series. BK Business titles pioneer new and progressive leadership and management practices in all types of public, private, and nonprofit organizations. They promote socially responsible approaches to business, innovative organizational change methods, and more humane and effective organizations.

FSC
www.fsc.org
MIX
Paper from
responsible sources
FSC® C012752